GCSE GEOGRAPHY-
QUESTIONS AND

JOHN GREENLEES

Hodder & Stoughton

A MEMBER OF THE HODDER HEADLINE GROUP

ACKNOWLEDGEMENTS

The author and the publishers would like to thank the Bridgeman Art Library for their permission to reproduce Figure 7.1A.

All other photographs were provided by the author, John Greenlees

The publishers would like to thank Ordnance Survey for their permission to reproduce Ordnance Survey material.

Every effort has been made to contact the holders of copyright material used in this book, but if any have been overlooked, the publishers will be pleased to make the necessary alterations at the first opportunity.

Orders: please contact Bookpoint Ltd, 39 Milton Park, Abingdon, Oxon OX14 4TD. Telephone: (44) 01235 400414, Fax: (44) 01235 400454. Lines are open from 9.00–6.00, Monday to Saturday, with a 24 hour message answering service. Email address: orders@bookpoint.co.uk

British Library Cataloguing in Publication Data
A catalogue record for this title is available from The British Library

ISBN 0 340 72547 8

First published 1999

Impression number	10	9	8	7	6	5	4	3	2	1
Year	2004	2003	2002	2001	2000	1999				

Typeset by Wearset, Boldon, Tyne and Wear.
Printed in Great Britain for Hodder & Stoughton Educational, a division of Hodder Headline Plc, 338 Euston Road, London NW1 3BH by Scotprint Ltd, Musselburgh, Scotland.

Contents

TOPICS

INTRODUCTION

GCSE Geography: Questions and Skills provides over 250 exam-type questions to help develop knowledge and understanding of the core topics which make up GCSE Geography. The exam-type questions are grouped according to topic so that they can be used for classroom work, homework assignments, revision for class tests and revision for the final GCSE exam. For each of the topics there is a detailed glossary to outline the meaning of key words.

The exam-type questions also provide invaluable practice at analysing and interpreting the maps, diagrams, graphs, tables of statistics, sketches, photographs and other information sources which are used in exam questions. A section on key skills has been included to provide notes and advice on how to recognise these different information sources and how to describe, explain, interpret and evaluate the information they offer.

GCSE Geography: Questions and Skills also provides useful advice on how to answer exam questions. The section on 'worked examples' provides examples of good answers and poor answers along with markers' comments to show how one answer succeeds while another fails. The markers' comments also include useful advice about how to avoid making the sort of mistakes which lead to disappointing grades.

Each topic chapter has two sets of questions – Core and Extension. The Core questions are mainly 'Foundation Tier' questions while the Extension questions are mainly 'Higher Tier' questions.

MAPS

Extracting information from maps is one of the most important skills in GCSE Geography. The main types of maps used in GCSE Geography include:

- Ordnance Survey (OS) maps;
- location maps;
- distribution maps;
- choropleth maps;
- land-use maps;
- sphere of influence maps;
- flow maps;
- cartograms.

Ordnance Survey maps show many different landscape features including landforms, lakes, rivers, forests, settlements, transport routes, farms and factories. Map 1 on the inside front cover is an OS map of a rural landscape in Sussex in southern England while Map 2 on the inside back cover is an OS map of an urban landscape in the York area of northern England. Landscape features on maps can be divided into physical features and human features.

Physical features on OS maps include:

- landforms such as hills, mountains and valleys;
- drainage features such as rivers, lakes and marshland;
- vegetation such as coniferous forests, deciduous forests and mixed forests.

OS maps also provide information about the relief (height and shape) of the land. Height is shown by spot heights, triangulation pillars and contour lines. Spot heights and triangulation pillars give the exact height of the land in metres. Contour lines join places lying at the same height to provide an indication of the height of all parts of the map. On 1:50 000 maps contour lines are drawn at 10 metre intervals.

Contour lines also enable the shape of the land to be studied and for cross-sections to be drawn. Contour lines close together indicate steep slopes while contour lines which are far apart indicate gentle slopes. The absence of contour lines indicates flat land.

Human features on OS maps include:

- settlements such as single buildings, hamlets, villages, towns and cities;
- agricultural features such as farm buildings, drainage ditches, orchards and greenhouses;
- industrial features such as mines, mills, factories, oil storage facilities and industrial estates;
- transport routes such as roads, railways, canals, seaports and airports.

OS maps also provide clues about many aspects of the built-up landscape including the functions and ages of settlements and their different parts. The presence of harbours and docks, for example, is evidence of ports while settlements surrounded by farmland, and with good communications and many services, probably function as market towns.

Evidence of long-established settlements is provided by the presence of old buildings such as castles and forts. Information about the ages of different parts of cities can be taken from the street patterns: a rectangular or grid iron pattern, for example, indicates an older part of a settlement while curved streets and cul-de-sacs indicate newer areas.

The central business district of a large town or city can be identified by the presence of features such as a town hall, a principal railway station and a coach station.

Evidence of measures which have been taken to reduce traffic congestion includes inner ring roads, outer ring roads, bypass roads and relief roads to reduce the number of cars going into the city-centre.

Location maps show the site and situation of a place or group of places. Map 3 is a location map which shows the site and situation of Bristol.

Distribution maps show the spread or distribution of places. Map 4 shows the distribution of Japan's largest cities.

Choropleth maps use different types of shading to show variations in, for example, rainfall or average family incomes. The lighter shadings usually indicate lower densities and numbers while the

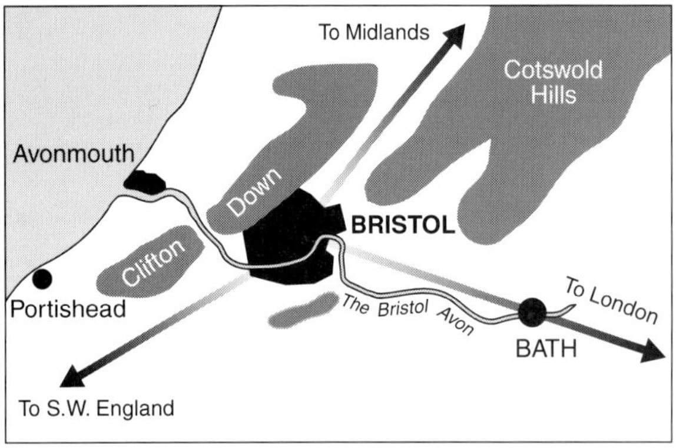

Map 3 A location map showing the site and situation of Bristol

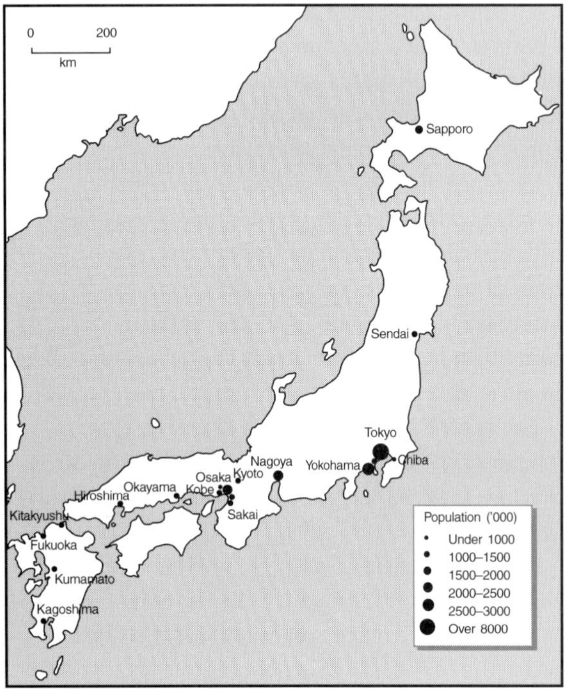

Map 4 The distribution of Japan's largest cities

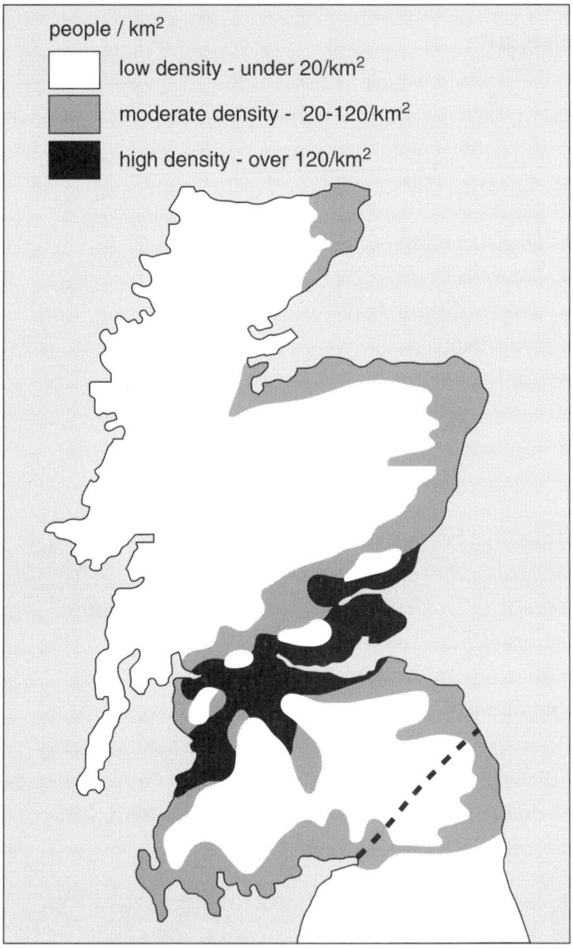

Map 5 A choropleth map showing variations in population density in Scotland

darker shadings usually indicate higher densities and numbers. Map 5 is a choropleth map which shows variations in population density in Scotland.

Isopleth maps use isolines to show places with equal values. Examples of isolines include contour lines (which join places lying at the same height), isobars (which join places with the same air pressure) and isotherms (which join places with the same temperature). Map 6 is an isopleth map which uses isotherms to show temperature variations in London.

Land-use maps show the main uses of land in an area such as the centre of a city, an industrial concentration or a farming area. Map 7 is a land-use map which shows the main uses of land in Liverpool.

Sphere of influence maps show the catchment areas or spheres of influence of services or settlements. Map 8 shows the spheres of influence of rural settlements in north east England.

Flow maps use lines and arrows to show links and movements. The widths of the lines are usually drawn in proportion to the volume of flow – thicker lines mean greater volumes of flow. The lines and

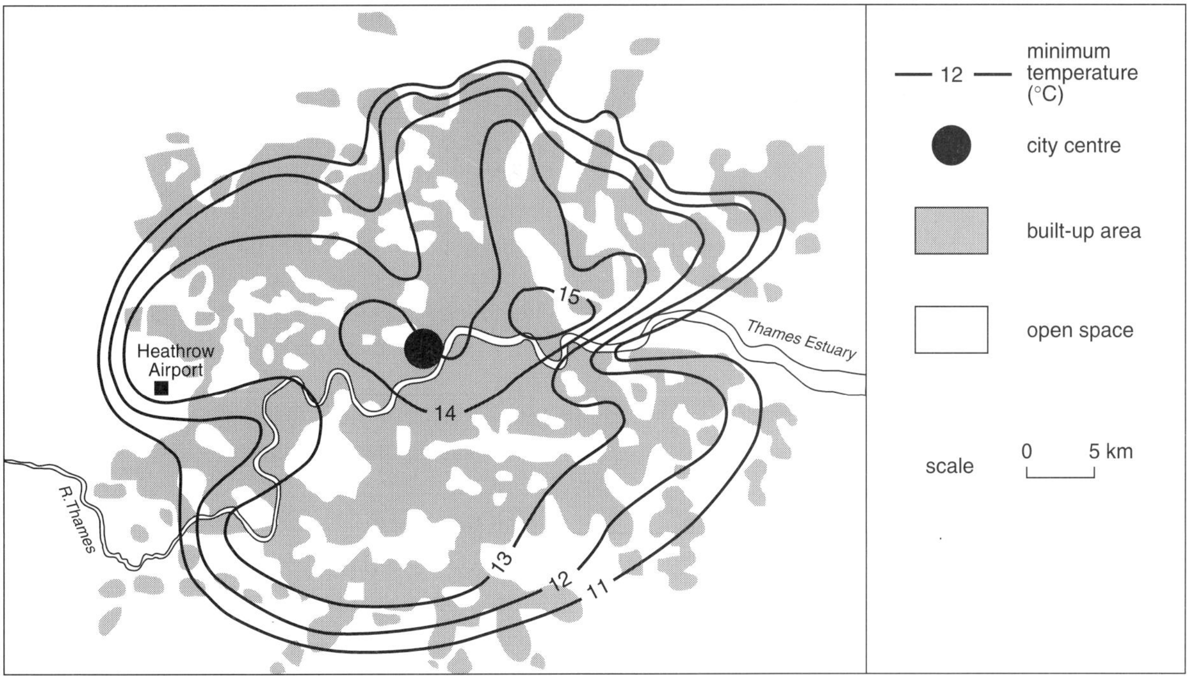

Map 6 An isopleth map showing temperature variations in London

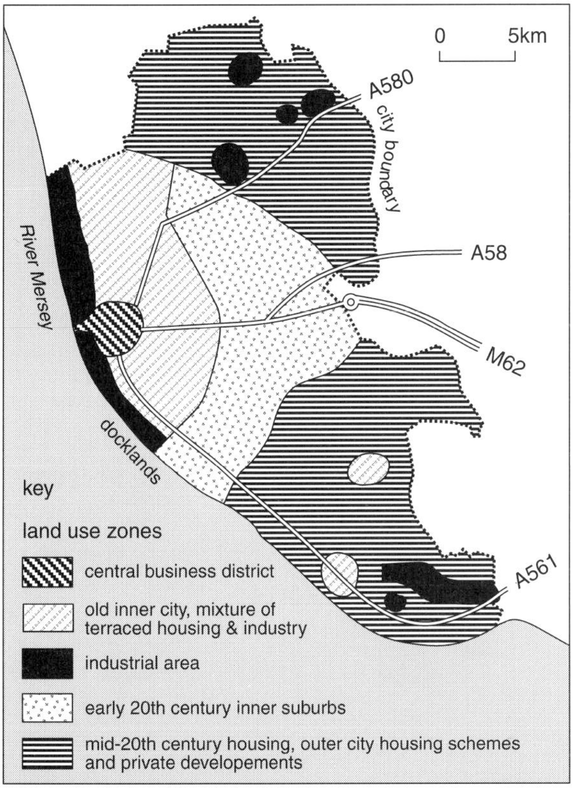

Map 7 A land-use map showing the main uses of land in Liverpool

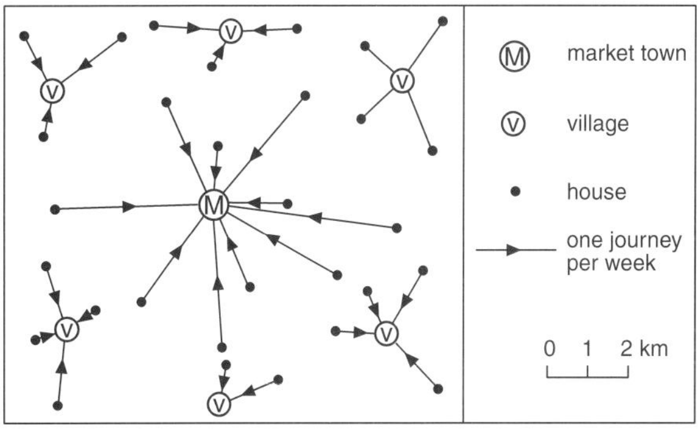

Map 8 The spheres of influence of rural settlements in north east England

arrows also show the general direction of movement. Map 9 is a flow map which shows the source and volume of visitors to the Yorkshire Dales National Park.

Cartograms are map diagrams which highlight particular features such as the population of different countries or regions. Countries or regions are drawn to a scale which isn't dependent on the actual size of the country or region. Map 10 is a cartogram which shows the regions of the world in proportion to the size of their populations.

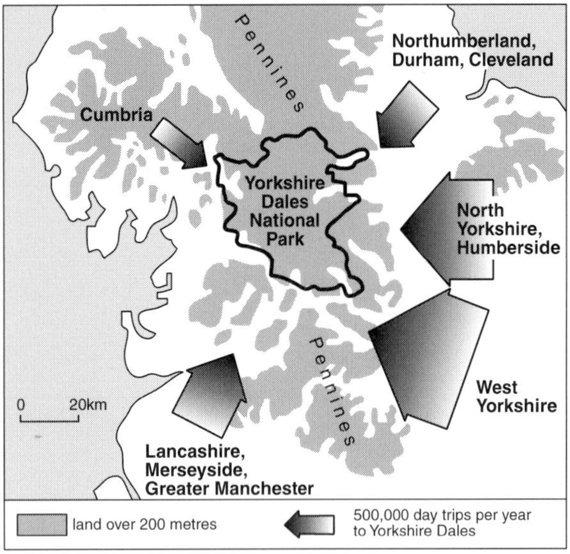

Map 9 A flow map showing the source and volume of visitors to the Yorkshire Dales National Park

Advice for interpreting maps

- look at the title of the map, if there is one, to find out what the map shows;
- use the key of the map to help you identify the different symbols and abbreviations;
- (with OS maps) use the contour lines, spot heights and triangulation pillars to work out the general height of the land (low-lying, moderate height and high land) as well as its shape (flat land, gentle slopes, moderate slopes, steep slopes, etc.);
- use the scale of the map to help you work out the real distances between places.

Worked example 1

Question: Describe the relief of the area to the west of easting 55 on Map 1 on the inside front cover.

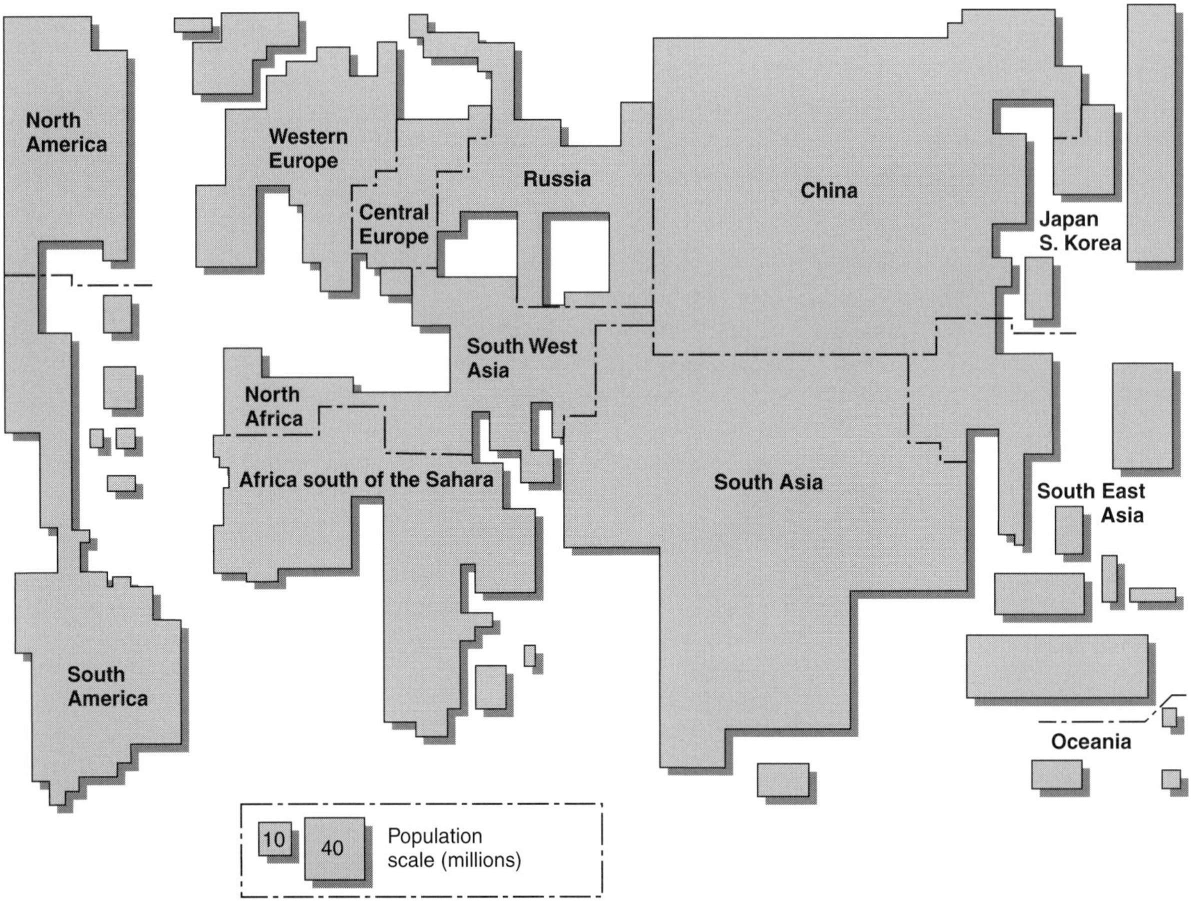

Map 10 A cartogram showing the population of the world's different regions

Answer: The land to the west of easting 55 includes steeply-sloping land which rises to a height of 214 metres at grid reference 548034. Lower ground is provided by the flat bottom of the valley of the Cuckmere River which lies at heights of less than 10 metres. The range of altitude in the map area is therefore around 200 metres. Landforms in the area include hills such as Windover Hill to the east of Alfriston, the valley of the Cuckmere River and a number of dry valleys (at grid reference 5300 for example). At the coast there is a series of cliffs including the 'Seven Sisters'.

Worked example 2

Question: Describe the site of York on Map 2 on the inside back cover.

Answer: York lies on flat and gently sloping land at the confluence of two rivers. The land is generally low-lying at heights of below 30 metres. York has a nucleated shape.

Practice activities

1 Use Map 1 on the inside front cover to give the grid reference of:

- **(a)** an area of low-lying ground;
- **(b)** an area of higher ground;
- **(c)** an area of flat land;
- **(d)** an area of gentle slopes;
- **(e)** an area of moderate slopes;
- **(f)** an area of steep slopes;
- **(g)** cliffs;
- **(h)** a river;
- **(i)** a confluence of two rivers;
- **(j)** a tributary;
- **(k)** a meander;
- **(l)** a flood plain;
- **(m)** a drainage ditch;
- **(n)** a dry valley;
- **(o)** a gap;
- **(p)** a beach.

2 Use Map 2 on the inside back cover to give the grid reference of:

- **(a)** a large settlement;
- **(b)** a small settlement;
- **(c)** an industrial area;
- **(d)** a farming area;
- **(e)** a service;
- **(f)** a tourist attraction;
- **(g)** an old street pattern with a grid-iron street layout;
- **(h)** a new street pattern with cul-de-sacs;
- **(i)** an inner ring road;
- **(j)** an outer ring road.

3 Use Map 3 to help you describe the site and situation of Bristol.

4 Describe the distribution of Japan's largest cities as shown by Map 4.

5 Use Map 5 to help you describe variations in population density in Scotland.

6 Use Map 6 to help you describe temperature variations in London.

7 Use Map 7 to help you describe the land-use of Liverpool.

8 Describe the spheres of influence of the rural settlements shown by Map 8.

9 Use Map 9 to help you describe the volume and source of visitors to the Yorkshire Dales National Park.

10 Use Map 10 to help you describe the populations of the world's different regions.

GRAPHS

A number of different types of graphs are used in GCSE Geography. These include:

- line graphs;
- bar graphs;
- compound graphs;
- pie charts and dissected bar graphs;
- scatter graphs.

Line graphs show changes or trends over a period of time, for example the change in the population of a place or the change in the price of wheat. Graph 1 is a line graph which shows changes to the world's population. Group line graphs include more than one line to enable comparisons to be made.

Bar graphs are used to show comparisons of, for example, different places at different times. Graph 2 is a bar graph which compares population change for six of the world's largest cities.

Compound graphs use lines and bars to show two different features. Graph 3 is a compound graph which shows the temperature and rainfall of Majorca in Spain.

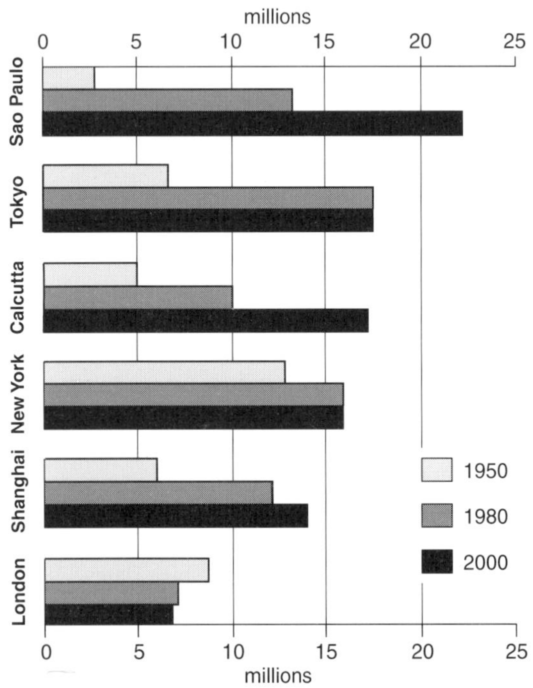

Graph 2 A bar graph showing population change for six of the world's largest cities

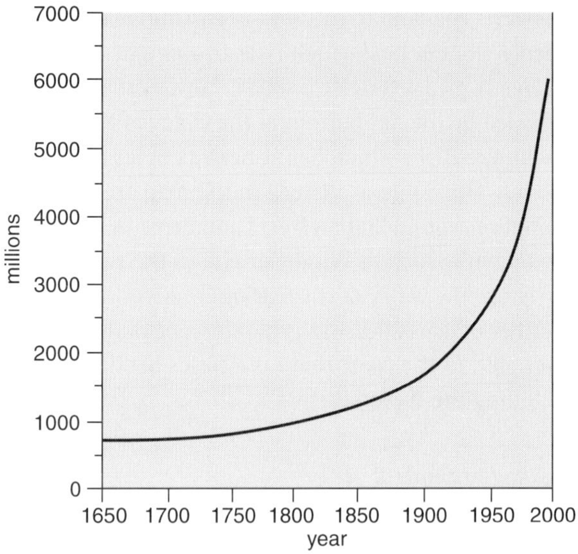

Graph 1 A line graph showing changes to the world's population

Pie charts and dissected bar graphs show the relative importance of different parts of a total. Graph 4 is a dissected bar graph which shows the relative importance of different land-uses in the central business district of Birmingham.

Scatter graphs show links and relationships. Graph 5 is a scatter graph which shows the relationship between the size of settlements and the number of services in the settlements.

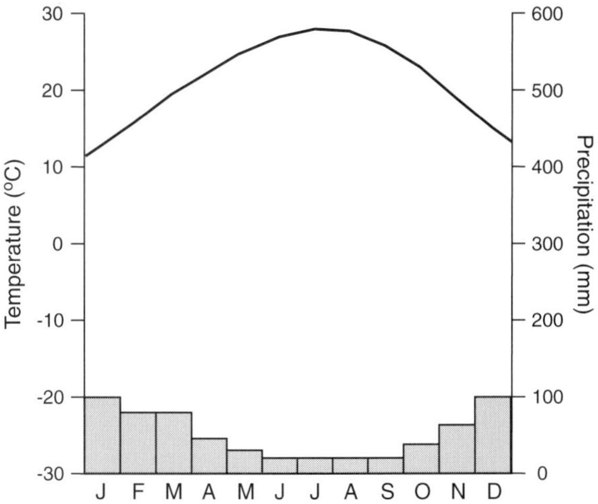

Graph 3 A compound graph showing the temperature and rainfall of Majorca

Advice for extracting information from graphs

- read the title of the graph to find out what the graph shows;
- read the information along the sides of the graph to identify the unit of measurement involved – remember to use this unit of measurement if you include any figures from the graph in your answer;
- the total area of pie charts or dissected bar diagrams equals 100 per cent – so half the area will equal 50 per cent, a quarter equals 25 per cent and a tenth equals 10 per cent;
- try and identify the changes, patterns or trends shown by the graph.

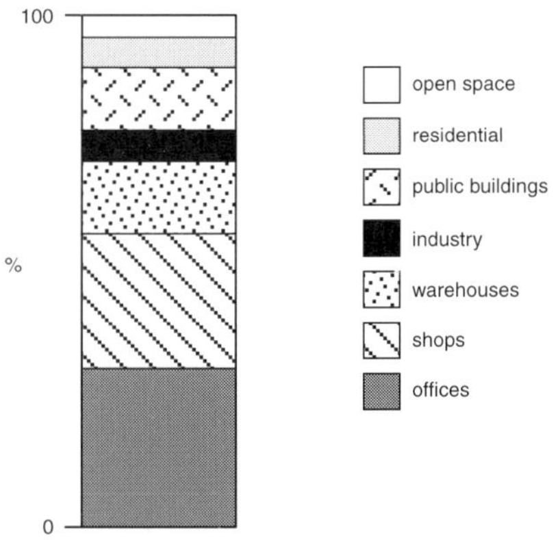

Graph 4 A dissected bar graph showing the different land-uses in the central business district of Birmingham

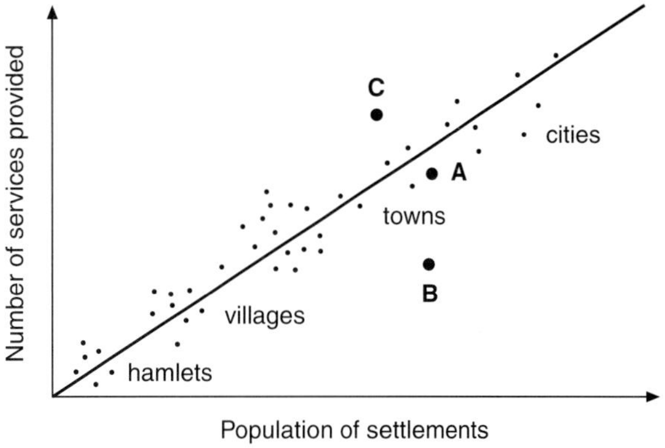

Graph 5 A scatter graph showing the relationship between the size of settlements and the number of services in the settlements

Worked example

Question: Use Graph 1 to help you describe changes in the population of the world between 1650 and today.

Answer: The world's population stayed at a very low level until around 1850 when it started to increase rapidly. In 1850 the population of the world was around 1000 million. By the year 1950 the population of the world had increased to almost 3000 million. Today the population of the world is over 6000 million.

Practice activities

1. Use Graph 2 to help you compare population change in six of the world's largest cities.
2. Use Graph 3 to help you describe the temperature and rainfall of Majorca.
3. Use Graph 4 to help you describe the land-uses in the central business district of Birmingham.
4. Use Graph 5 to help you describe the relationship between the size of settlements and the number of services in the settlements.

PHOTOGRAPHS

A photograph shows an area as it actually is. The main types of photographs used in GCSE Geography are:

- satellite photographs of, for example, weather systems;
- aerial photographs (photographs taken from aircraft rather than satellites);
- ground photographs.

Advice for interpreting photographs

- look at the title of the photograph for information about what the photograph shows;
- examine the entire photograph and not just part of it;
- look for the dominant feature or features;
- look for links and relationships, for example: between the height of the land and the land-use;
- ask questions such as:
  - what does the photograph show?
  - what are the most important features of the photograph?
  - what are these features like?
  - why are these features like this?

Worked example

Question: Describe the main features of the area shown in Photograph 1.

Answer: Photograph 1 shows an urban area which lies next to a river or sea. Many of the buildings are old buildings including several churches with tall spires. The streets are narrow which also suggests that this is an old area. Evidence of newer buildings, and port facilities, can be seen in the background of the photograph.

Practice activity

Describe the main features of the area shown in Photograph 2.

Photograph 1 An urban area

Photograph 2

FIELD-SKETCHES

Field-sketches show the main features of an area. Only information which is directly linked to the study-topic is usually included in the sketch. Annotations or labels are usually included to give additional information about the sketch's most important features. Field-sketch 1 shows an annotated field-sketch of a hydro-electric power scheme.

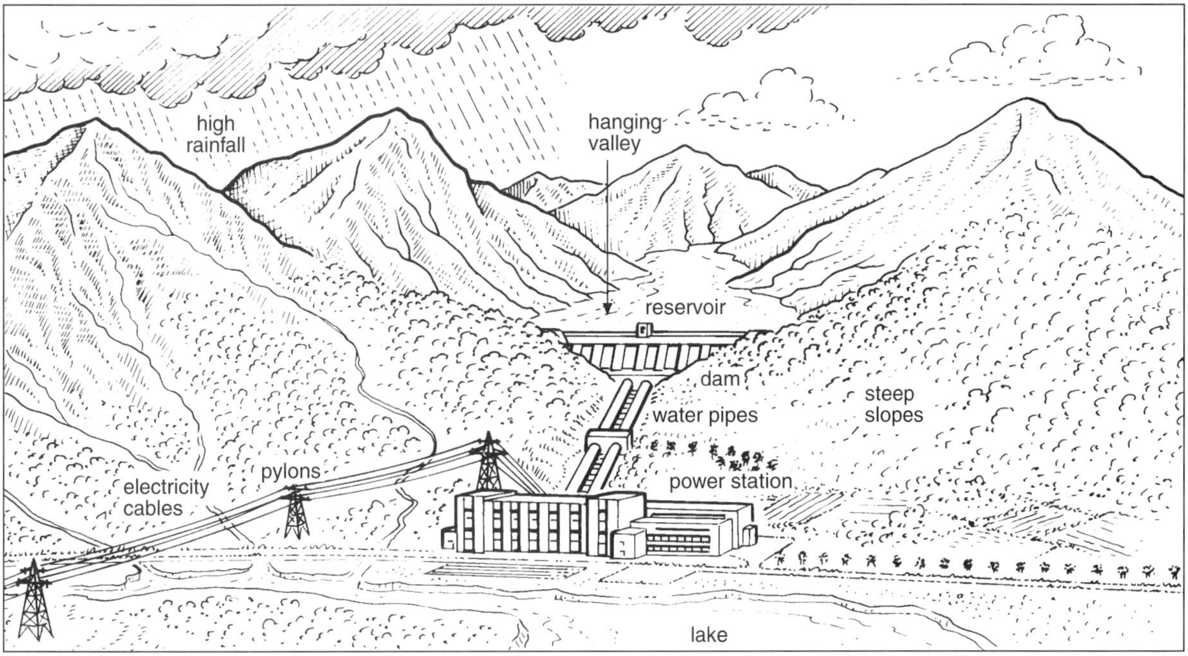

Field-sketch 1 A hydro-electric power scheme

Advice for interpreting field-sketches

- look at the title of the field-sketch for information about what the field-sketch shows;
- examine the entire field-sketch and not just part of it;
- read the information provided by the labels and annotations;
- look for the dominant feature or features;
- look for links and relationships, for example: between the height of the land and the land-use;
- ask questions such as:
  - what does the field-sketch show?
  - what are the most important features of the field-sketch?
  - what are these features like?
  - why are these features like this?

Worked example

Question: Use Field-sketch 1 to help you describe the different parts of a hydro-electric power scheme.

Answer: The hydro-electric power scheme includes a dam which has been built across a hanging valley in a mountainous area. The dam has created a reservoir which supplies water, through water-pipes, to the power station. Inside the power station the water is used to turn turbines and thereby generate electricity. Water from the power station flows into another lake. The electricity is transmitted to settlements by cables held up by pylons.

Practice activity

Draw an annotated field-sketch showing the site and situation of Corfe Castle (as shown in Photograph 3).

Photograph 3 Corfe Castle

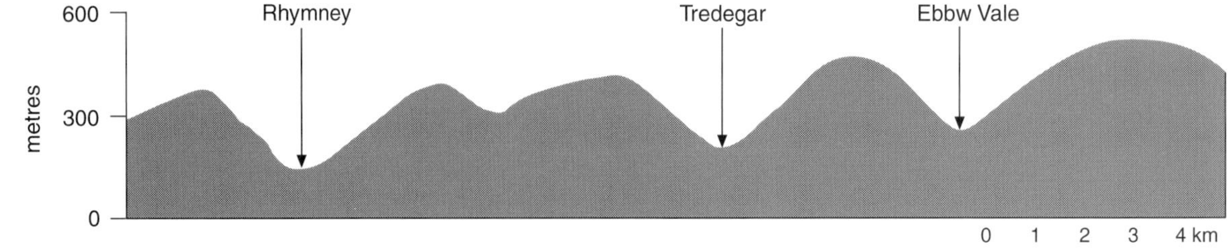

Diagram 1 A cross-section from Rhymney to Ebbw Vale

DIAGRAMS

The diagrams used in GCSE Geography include cross-sections and transects.

A cross-section is a sideways view of an area of land which shows changes in the shape and height of the land. Cross-sections are also used to show the site and situation of a settlement or transport route in relation to land features such as mountains and valleys. Diagram 1 is a cross-section from Rhymney to Ebbw Vale in south Wales.

A transect is a cross-section with additional information listed below it. This additional information might include details about the rock-type, soil and land-use to allow influences and relationships to be shown. Diagram 2 is a transect which shows landforms, geology, soil and land-use in the landscape to the south of London.

Worked example

Question: Use Diagram 2 to help you describe the relationship between landforms, geology and land-use in the landscape to the south of London.

Answer: Areas of high relief are formed from harder rocks such as chalk and sandstone while areas of low relief are formed from softer clays. The lower slopes of the hills are used for arable farming while the upper slopes are used for sheep grazing. The highest and steepest slopes are used for woodland while the low-lying clay areas are used for settlements and dairy farming.

Practice activity

Use Diagram 1 to help you describe the relief of the land between Rhymney and Ebbw Vale.

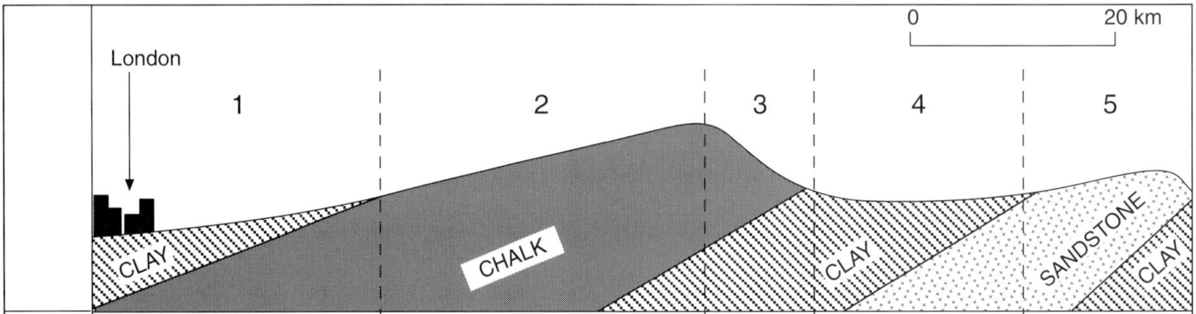

	1	2	3	4	5
Landforms	CLAY BASIN	CHALK DIP SLOPE	CHALK SCARP SLOPE	CLAY VALE	SANDSTONE RIDGE
Soil	Medium clays and loams	Clay with flints	Thin dry soils	Heavy clay	Thin sandy soils
Land use	Market gardening	Cereals, sheep, orchards on lower slopes	Woodland and some sheep	Dairying	Woodland, heath and rough pasture

Diagram 2 A transect of the landscape to the south of London

DESCRIBING

Describing involves stating what a landform, a project, a situation, a policy or some other subject is like. A good description will contain many facts and details about the subject, for example: the name, type, size, shape, height and structure of a landform. In exam questions describing enables you to reveal your knowledge of the topic concerned.

Here is an example of a 'describing' question and answer:

Question: Use Graph 6 to help you describe the changes in land-values across a city.

Answer: Land-values are very high in the central business district in the centre of the city. These values decrease rapidly at the edge of the CBD so that the old inner city is an area of low land-values. Outwards from the old inner city the land becomes slightly more expensive in the part of the city which has old but good quality housing. At the edge of the city the values decrease again.

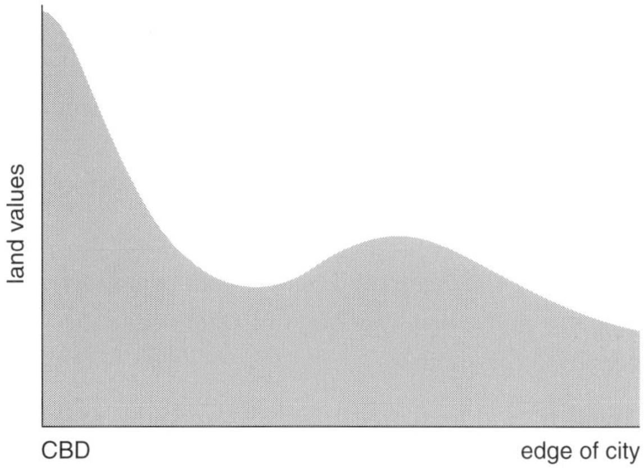

Graph 6 Changes in land-values across a city

Practice activity
Describe the coastal landscape shown in Photograph 4.

Advice for describing
Information sources such as maps, photographs, graphs and diagrams contain useful information which should be included in any descriptions you are asked to write. Make full use of this information and include relevant points and examples in your description.

Photograph 4 A coastal landscape

EXPLAINING

Explaining is giving reasons for the way something is, for example: why major earthquakes only occur in certain parts of the world.

Here is an example of an 'explaining' question and answer:

Question: Use Diagram 3 to help you explain the changes in the height of buildings from the city centre to the suburbs.

Answer: Buildings are highest in the centre of the city because this is the city's most expensive area of land. High buildings make the best possible use of expensive land. The height of buildings is much lower in the suburbs because the land is cheaper there and more space can be devoted to low-rise houses with gardens and garages.

Practice activity

Explain the different increases in population shown by Graph 7.

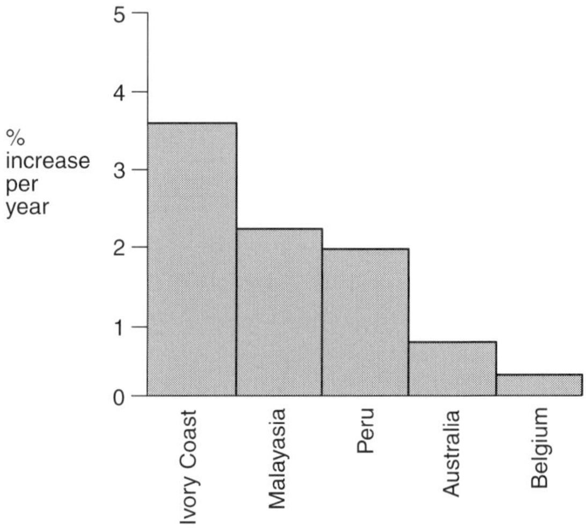

Graph 7 Population increase

Advice for explaining

Remember that explaining is *not* describing. With exam questions don't waste time describing something when a question only asks you to explain. Devote your time to giving the reasons the question asks for.

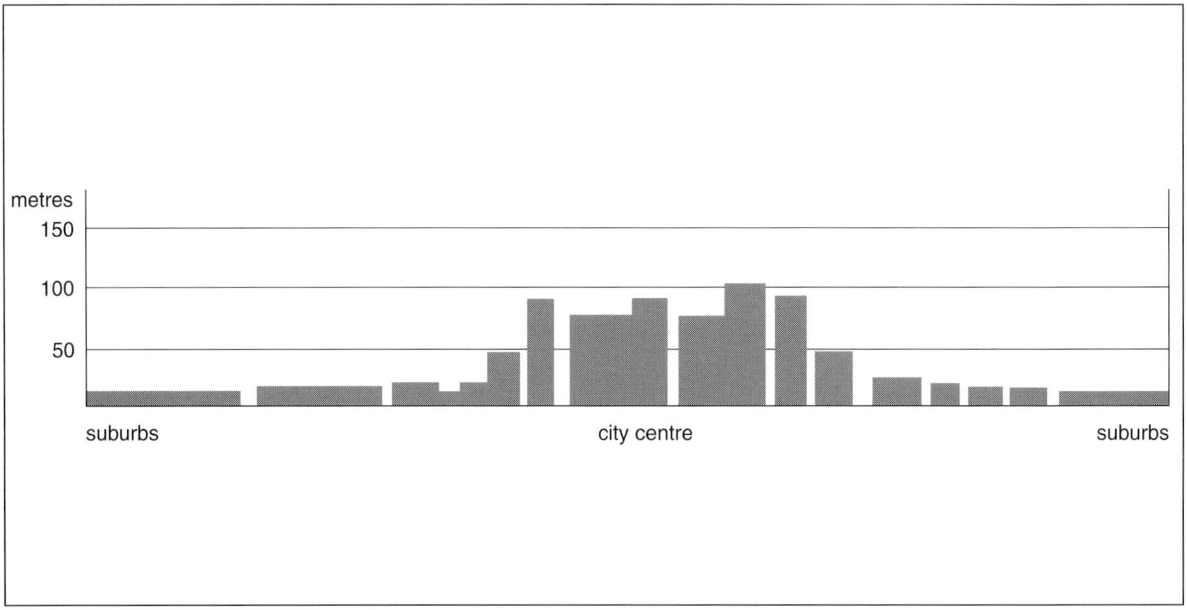

Diagram 3 Changes in the height of buildings from the city centre to the suburbs

INTERPRETING

Interpreting geographical data involves extracting information from an information source and then bringing out its full meaning.

Here is an example of an 'interpreting' question and answer:

Question: State the relationship between rainfall and river flow as shown by Graph 8.

Answer: The graph shows that river flow increases after a period of heavy rainfall. The increase in river flow occurs after a slight delay called 'lag time'. This is the time it takes for the water to run off the land into the rivers. In the case of Graph 8 the heaviest rainfall fell between 12 midnight on Monday and 8 am on Tuesday while the peak river flow occurred between 12 noon and 4 pm on Tuesday.

Practice activity
State the link between relief and land-use in the area shown in Photograph 5.

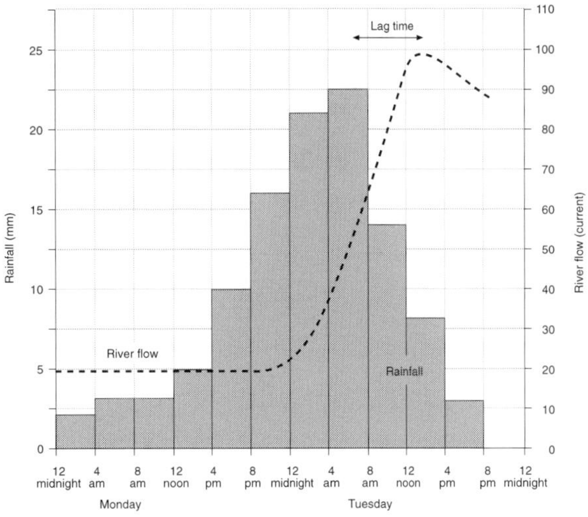

Graph 8 Changes in rainfall and river flow

Advice for interpreting
Make full use of the information which is included in the information source and add your own knowledge of the topic. For sketches, diagrams, graphs, photographs, etc., ask yourself questions such as 'what is being shown' and 'why is it this way'.

Photograph 5

EVALUATING

Evaluating geographical information involves assessing or judging the information and then making a valid conclusion.

Here is an example of an evaluating question and answer:

Question: Assess the advantages and disadvantages of the site of the coastal settlement shown in Photograph 6.

Answer: A major disadvantage of the site of the settlement shown in Photograph 6 is that the land is very steep which means building is more difficult and expensive. The steep slopes also make it more difficult to get from one part of the settlement to another. An advantage of the site of the settlement is that it lies next to the sea which will provide opportunities for many different activities including fishing and tourism. Although the steep site of this settlement creates problems the presence of the sea provides many advantages.

Practice activity

Assess the usefulness of the location of the industrial area shown in Photograph 7.

Photograph 7 An industrial area

Advice for evaluating

Try to give a balanced assessment which provides all sides of an issue. Remember to give a conclusion based on your assessment.

Photograph 6 A coastal settlement

1 Plate Tectonics

Key words

active volcano a volcano which is erupting or is likely to erupt; examples include Mount Vesuvius in Italy and Mount Pinatubo in the Philippines

cone volcano a volcano with a circular base which tapers to a point at the top

constructive margin the boundary between two plates which are moving apart (in other words they are diverging)

convergent plates crustal plates which are moving towards each other (in other words they are converging)

crater the top, usually circular, part of a volcanic cone

crustal plates the huge slabs of solid rock which make up the Earth's crust

destructive margin the boundary between two plates which are moving towards each other (converging); destructive or colliding margins are associated with intense compression and the formation of fold mountains, volcanoes and earthquakes

divergent plates plates which are pulling apart; this allows molten rock to rise up from the earth's interior

dormant volcano a volcano which hasn't erupted for a long period but which might still erupt in the future

earthquake a shaking of the ground caused by sudden movements in the Earth's crust

epicentre the point of the Earth's surface which is directly above the focus of an earthquake

extinct volcano a volcano which erupted in the past but will never erupt again

fault a fracture in the earth's crust; an example is the San Andreas Fault in California

focus the point of origin of an earthquake

fold mountains mountains formed by upward movements of the Earth's surface; many fold mountains are associated with the destructive margins of plates; examples of fold mountains include the Alps in Europe

geothermal energy energy produced by pumping water through joints in rocks which have been warmed by the natural heat of the Earth's interior; the hot water is then used to generate electricity; geothermal electricity is generated in countries such as Iceland and New Zealand

geyser natural springs, in areas of volcanic activity, which throw out jets of hot water and steam

igneous rocks rocks which form when molten lava or magma cools and becomes solid

lava the molten rock which flows out of a volcano

magma the molten rock inside a volcano

Mercalli Scale a scale for measuring the intensity of earthquakes

plate a large slab of the Earth's crust which floats on the semi-molten rock which lies below it

plate margin a boundary between crustal plates

plate tectonics the movement of the Earth's crustal plates which is linked to earthquakes, volcanoes and the formation of fold mountains

Richter Scale a scale which measures the magnitude of earthquakes

'Ring of Fire' the ring of volcanoes around the Pacific Ocean

San Andreas Fault a fault-line in California, USA, which marks the boundary between two crustal plates

shield volcano a broad, shallow volcano cone produced from free-flowing lava

tsunami a giant wave caused by an underwater earthquake

CORE QUESTIONS

1 (a) Figure 1.1A shows the Earth's crustal plates while Figure 1.1B shows the Earth's earthquake zones.
Name two crustal plates which meet at:
i. Japan;
ii. India. (2)

(b) Explain why major earthquakes occur in the zones marked in Figure 1.1B. (2)

(c) Outline the problems which would arise if a major earthquake was to occur in:
i. an urban area; (3)
ii. a rural area. (3)

(d) Study Figure 1.1C.
Why do earthquakes in poorer countries such as India often result in a higher number of deaths than earthquakes in richer countries such as Japan? (2)

(e) i. Name two organisations which would provide help for areas affected by major earthquakes. (2)
ii. Describe the sort of help which each of these organisations would be able to provide. (2)

Figure 1.1C Major earthquake disasters

location	year	magnitude	number of deaths
China	1927	8.3	200 000
China	1976	7.8	240 000
India	1934	8.4	11 000
India	1935	7.5	30 000
Japan	1995	7.2	5000
USA	1906	8.3	452
USA	1985	7.1	62

(f) Describe two measures which can be taken to try and protect people from the effects of earthquakes. (4)

(20)

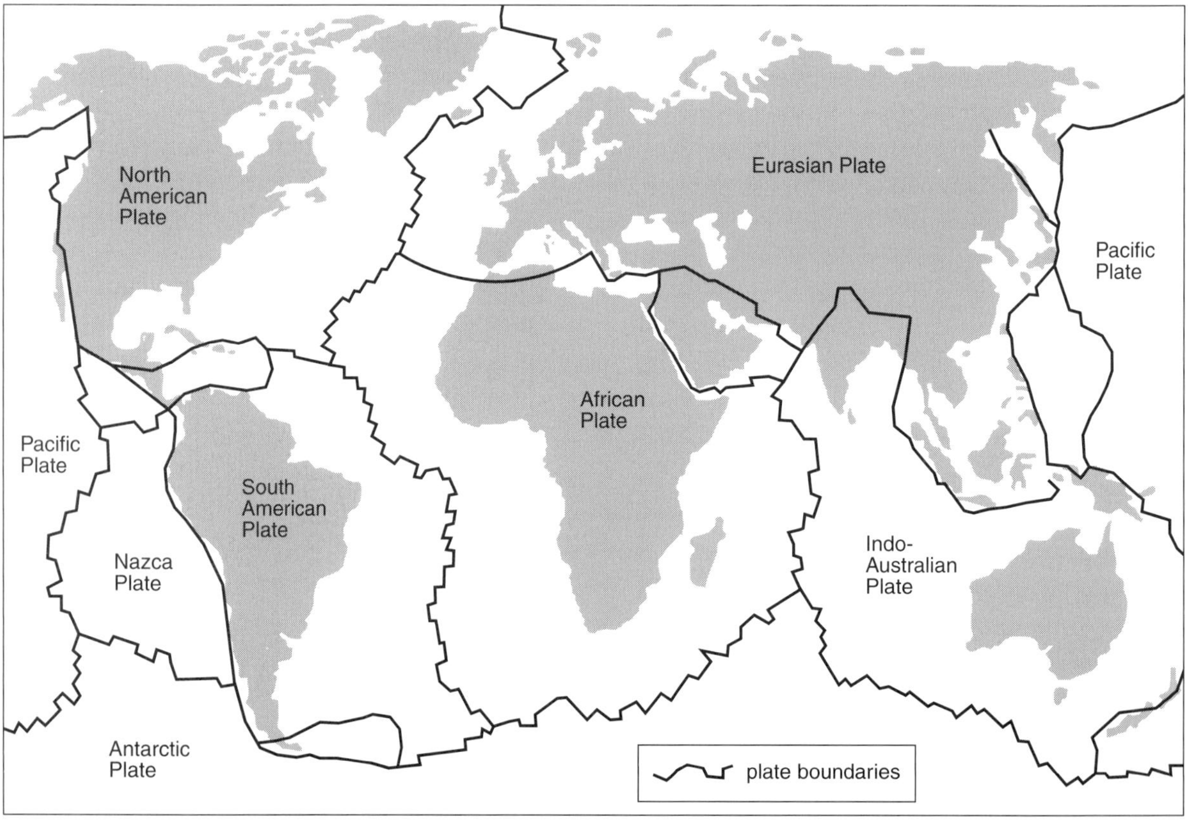

Figure 1.1A The Earth's main crustal plates

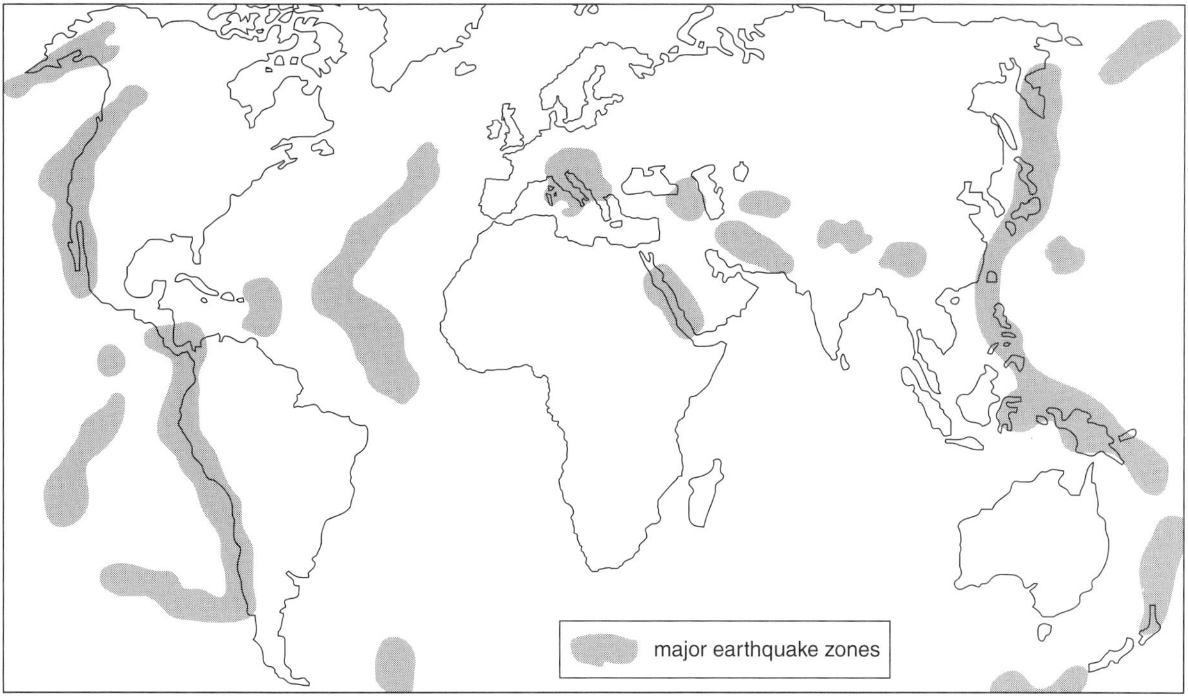

Figure 1.1B The world's most important earthquake zones

2 (a) Examine Figure 1.2A which shows a cross-section of a volcano. Copy the cross-section and then label the following:

crater
magma chamber
lava
vent (4)

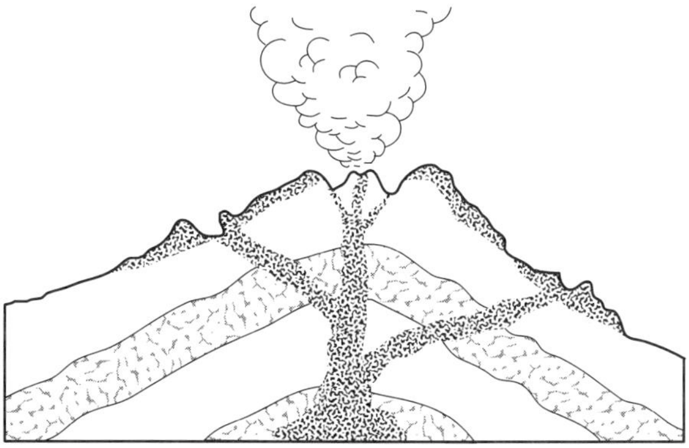

Figure 1.2A A cross-section of a volcano

(b) Look at Figure 1.2B which shows an extinct volcano.
Outline the difference between active, dormant and extinct volcanoes. (3)

(c) Describe the hazards associated with active volcanoes. (3)

(d) Give reasons why people, in spite of the dangers, continue to live in areas affected by volcanic activity. (4)

Figure 1.2B An extinct volcano

(e) Figure 1.2C shows the 'Ring of Fire'.

i. Outline what is meant by the 'Ring of Fire'. (2)

ii. Explain why there are so many volcanoes around the Pacific Ocean. (4)

(20)

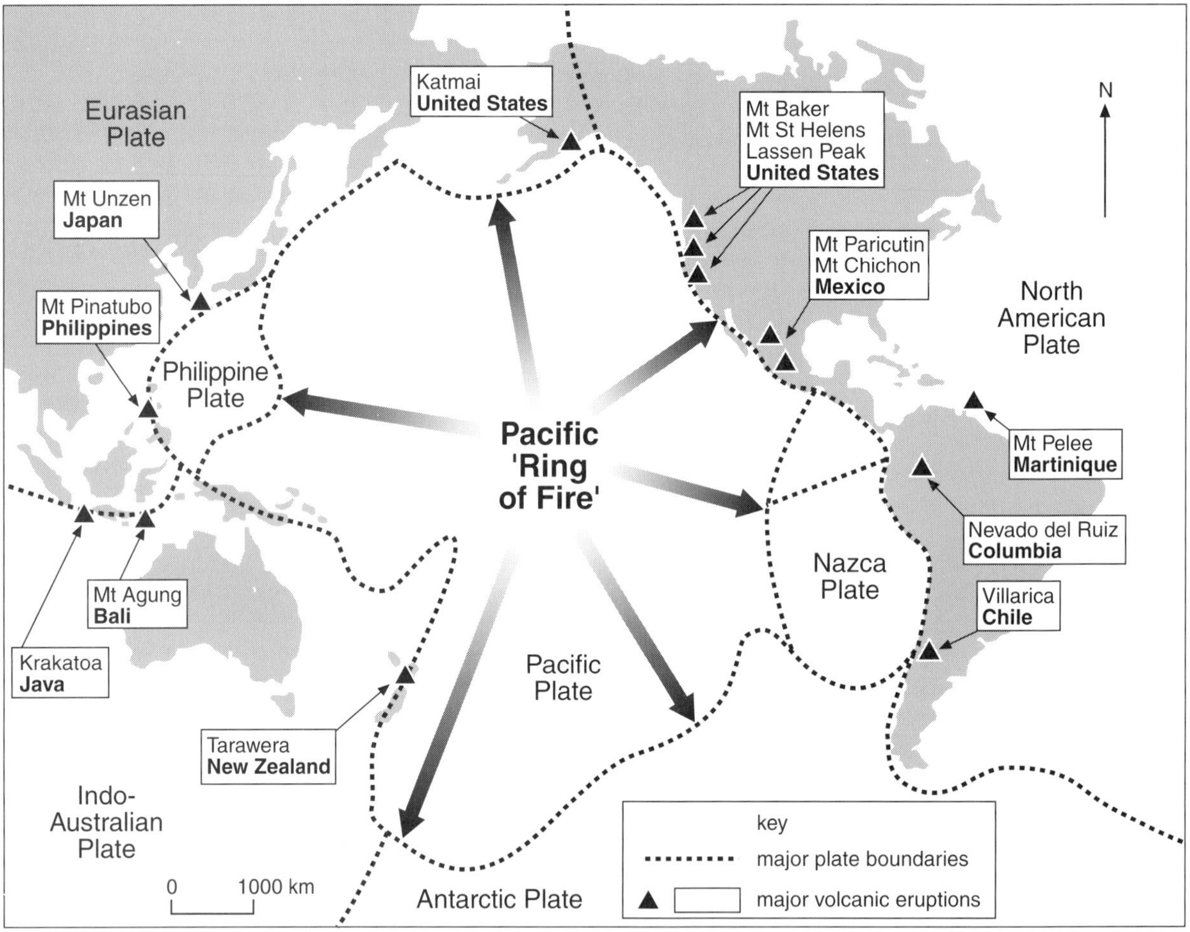

Figure 1.2C The 'Ring of Fire'

3 (a) Examine Figure 1.3A which shows part of a newspaper report about the Kobe Earthquake of 1995.

i. Give three reasons why so many people died in this earthquake. (3)

ii. What prevented the death toll being even higher? (2)

iii. Give two examples of the type of short term aid Kobe would have required. (2)

iv. Give two examples of the type of long term aid Kobe would have required. (2)

(b) Figure 1.3B and Figure 1.3C show two photographs of Kobe after the earthquake. Why did some parts of Kobe suffer more damage than other parts? (4)

(c) Figure 1.3D shows three newspaper headlines about volcanic eruptions in Japan and Italy. Explain why countries like Japan and Italy experience earthquakes as well as volcanoes. (3)

(d) Outline what happened during a major volcanic eruption you have studied. (4)

(20)

Over 5000 people died after an earthquake devastated the city of Kobe in West Japan. Large parts of the city were engulfed in flames as fire quickly spread from one house to another. The 20-second earthquake, whose focus was on nearby Awaji Island, took place at 5:46 in the morning. The elevated Kanto Expressway was toppled and railway tracks buckled by the tremor which measured 7.2 on the Richter Scale. A large part of the port area was destroyed and many factories suffered major damage. In the centre of the city the Sogo department store was split apart.

Figure 1.3A Part of a newspaper report

Figure 1.3B Earthquake damage, Kobe

Figure 1.3C Earthquake damage, Kobe

ANOTHER ETNA ERUPTION DEVASTATES THE LANDSCAPE

ASH FROM MOUNT UNZEN RAINS DOWN ON PRIMARY SCHOOL

LAVA FLOWS FROM VESUVIUS DESTROY FARMLAND AND SETTLEMENTS

Figure 1.3D Newspaper headlines about volcanic eruptions in Japan and Italy

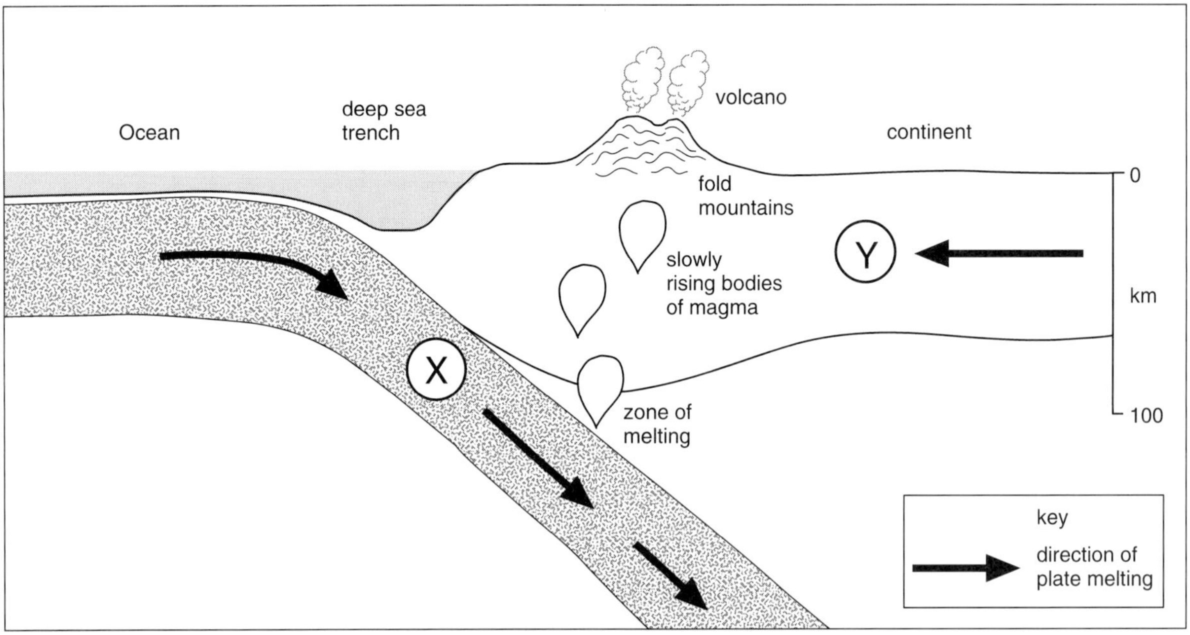

Figure 1.4A The margins of the earth's crustal plates

EXTENSION QUESTIONS

4 (a) Study Figure 1.4A which shows the margins of the Earth's crustal plates.

i. What is a 'crustal plate'? (2)

ii. Describe what is happening at X and Y. (5)

(b) State the meaning of the terms 'focus of an earthquake' and 'epicentre of an earthquake'. (2)

(c) Figure 1.4B shows the seismic waves which accompanied the Lisbon Earthquake of 1755. Describe and explain the effects of the Lisbon Earthquake. (4)

(d) Using named examples explain why the most powerful earthquakes don't always cause the greatest damage and loss of life. (6)

(e) Examine Figure 1.4C which shows the effects of an underwater earthquake. Account for the sort of damage which sometimes results from underwater earthquakes. (6)

(25)

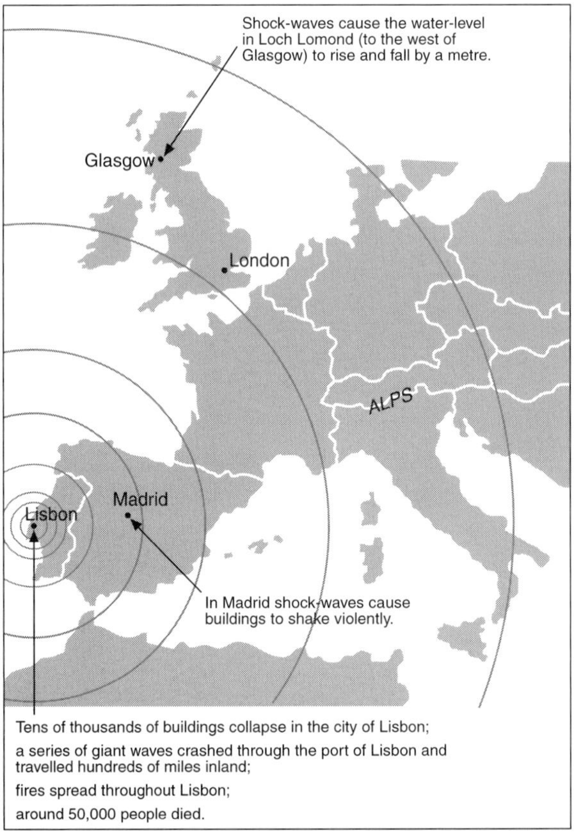

Figure 1.4B The seismic waves which accompanied the Lisbon Earthquake of 1755

Figure 1.4C A sketch showing the effects of an underwater earthquake

5 (a) Using named examples outline the effects that major volcanic eruptions can have on:

i. the landscape; (3)
ii. the local people; (3)
iii. the weather. (3)

(b) Examine Figure 1.5A which shows tourists on Mount Vesuvius. Discuss the different ways that volcanoes have economic value. (6)

Figure 1.5A Tourists on Mount Vesuvius

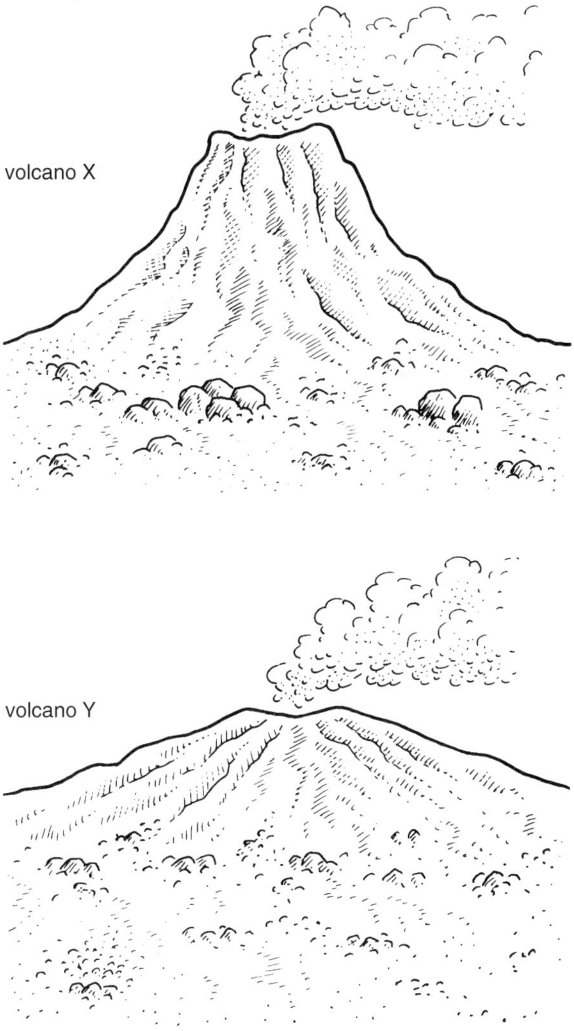

Figure 1.5B Two different volcanoes

(c) Figure 1.5B shows two different volcanoes. Describe and explain the different shapes of these two volcanoes. (6)

(d) Explain the cause of a recent eruption. (4)

(25)

6 (a) Examine Figure 1.6A which shows the relationship between earthquake intensity and the number of deaths for eight earthquakes.

i. Which earthquake had the lowest magnitude but the highest number of deaths? (1)

ii. Why do earthquakes of low magnitude sometimes result in a high number of deaths? (2)

iii. Which earthquake had a magnitude of 6.9 but a low number of deaths? (1)

iv. Why do earthquakes of high magnitude not always result in a high number of deaths? (2)

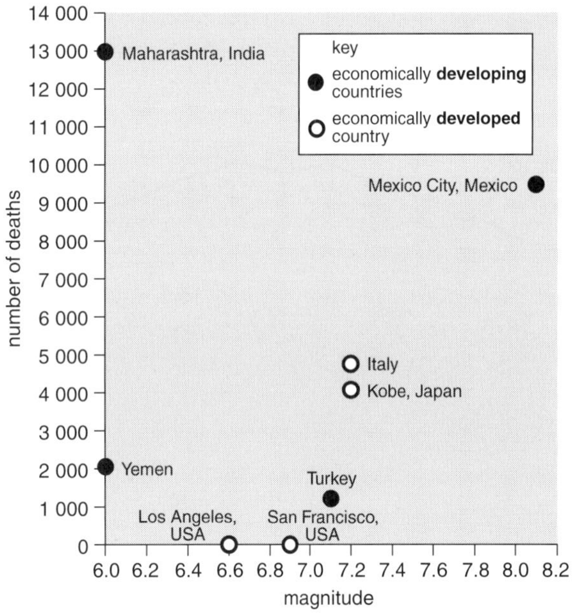

Figure 1.6A The relationship between earthquake intensity and the number of deaths for eight earthquakes

(b) Study Figure 1.6B which shows the San Andreas Fault in California, USA.

i. Explain why faults such as the San Andreas are responsible for earthquakes. (4)

ii. Describe and explain the impact of a major earthquake disaster you have studied. (5)

iii. Explain why people continue to live in areas affected by earthquakes. (4)

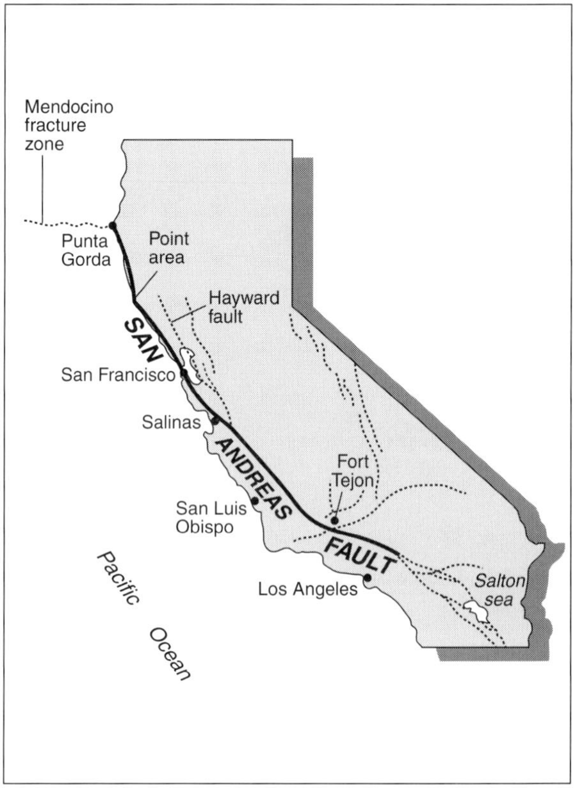

Figure 1.6B The San Andreas Fault

(c) Figure 1.6C is an extract from a magazine article.

Referring to named examples from different parts of the economically developed world outline the measures which can be taken to lessen the impact of earthquakes. (6)

(25)

In Tokyo the first day of September is 'Disaster Day'. This was the day back in 1923 when the Great Kanto Earthquake destroyed much of the city and killed over 90 000 people. Today 'Disaster Day' is a day when people take part in earthquake drills so that they know what to do, and where to go, if another 'Big One' shakes the city.

Figure 1.6C An extract from a magazine article

2 Rivers

Key words

alluvium the mud and silt deposited by rivers
aquifer a layer of rock which can hold water
attrition a form of erosion which is caused by pebbles repeatedly hitting against each other to become smaller and more rounded
basin lag the time difference between peak rainfall and peak river-flow
braiding the division of a river into two or more streams
catchment area the area drained by a river and its tributaries
condensation the change of water from vapour to liquid
confluence a point where two rivers meet
corrasion a form of erosion which is caused by particles scraping against the bed and sides of a river
delta the silt deposited at the mouth of a river; this happens after the river loses power and has to deposit its load
deposition the dropping of material which has been eroded and transported
discharge the quantity of water which flows past a fixed point in a river during a certain period
drainage basin the area drained by a river and its tributaries
erosion the wearing down and removal of rock
floodplain the wide, flat plain formed when a river deposits its load in its lower course
ground water all the water which seeps underground into the spaces in rocks; ground water moves slowly to rivers and the oceans
hydraulic action a form of erosion which is caused by the force of moving water
hydrograph a graph which shows the record of channel flow in a river or stream
impermeable rock a rock which water can't pass through
infiltration the process of water soaking into the ground; the infiltration rate is the speed at which water soaks into the ground
interception the ability of plants and objects, such as buildings, to store water for short periods
levees natural embankments formed by the deposition of silt when a river floods
meander a bend or curve in a river
ox-bow lake a small crescent-shaped lake formed after a river erodes the outside bend of a meander so that the neck of the meander becomes narrow enough for the river to break through; the deposition of sediment results in the ox-bow lake being cut off from the river
permeable rock a rock which water can pass through
point bar the deposition of sand and gravel on the inside of a meander loop
regime the pattern of seasonal variations in the volume of water in a river
runoff rain-water running off from where it falls
solution a form of erosion which involves rivers dissolving minerals in the rocks they flow over
suspension a form of transportation in which small rock particles are carried within the river
terraces the remains of former floodplains through which the river has cut
transpiration the process by which plants lose water
transportation the movement of material in rivers by suspension and solution
tributary a river which joins another river
watershed the boundary of a drainage basin

CORE QUESTIONS

1 (a) Figure 2.1A shows the catchment area of a river.
Which letter (A, B, C or D) marks:
i. the source of the river;
ii. the mouth of the river;
iii. a tributary of the main river;
iv. the watershed of the catchment area? (4)

(b) Figure 2.1B shows rainfall during one month while Figure 2.1C shows the discharge of a river during the same month.
i. What is meant by the 'discharge' of a river? (1)
ii. Describe the discharge of the river shown in Figure 2.1C. (3)
iii. Outline the link between rainfall and discharge. (2)

(c) Figure 2.1D shows flooding in the centre of York.
i. For York, or any other area you have studied, describe the causes of flooding. (3)
ii. Describe the effects of a named flood you have studied. (4)
iii. Outline two different measures which can be taken to prevent a river from flooding. (3)

(20)

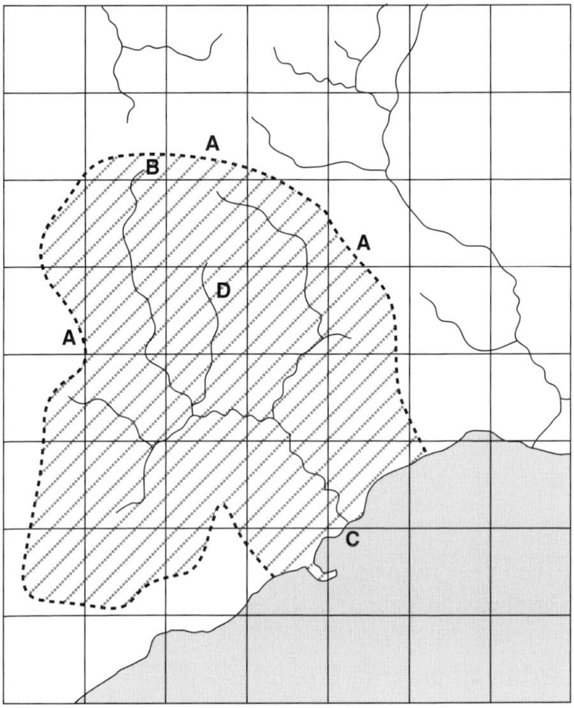

Figure 2.1A The catchment area of a river

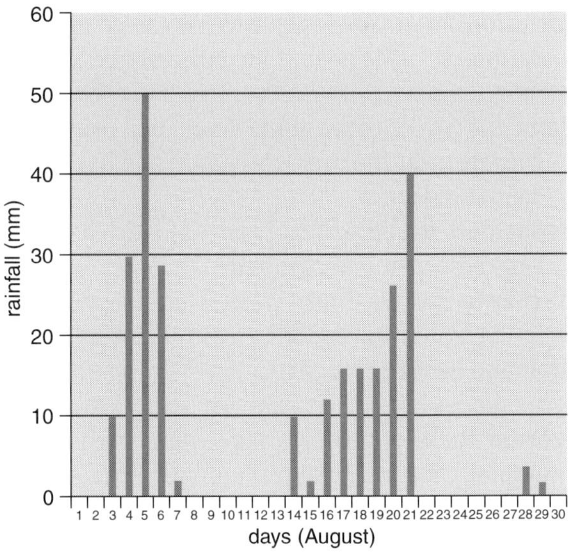

Figure 2.1B Rainfall during one month

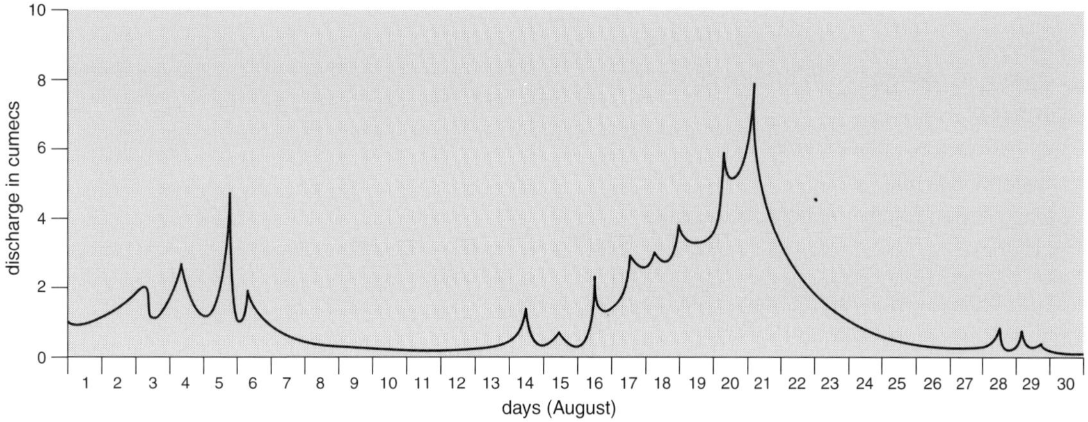

Figure 2.1C The discharge of a river

2 (a) Figure 2.2A shows the flow of two rivers (X and Y) over a year.

i. State two differences between the flow of these two rivers. (2)

ii. State the month when River Y had its peak discharge. Give a reason for your choice. (2)

iii. Which of the two rivers is more likely to flood? Give a reason for your choice. (2)

Figure 2.1D Flooding in the centre of York

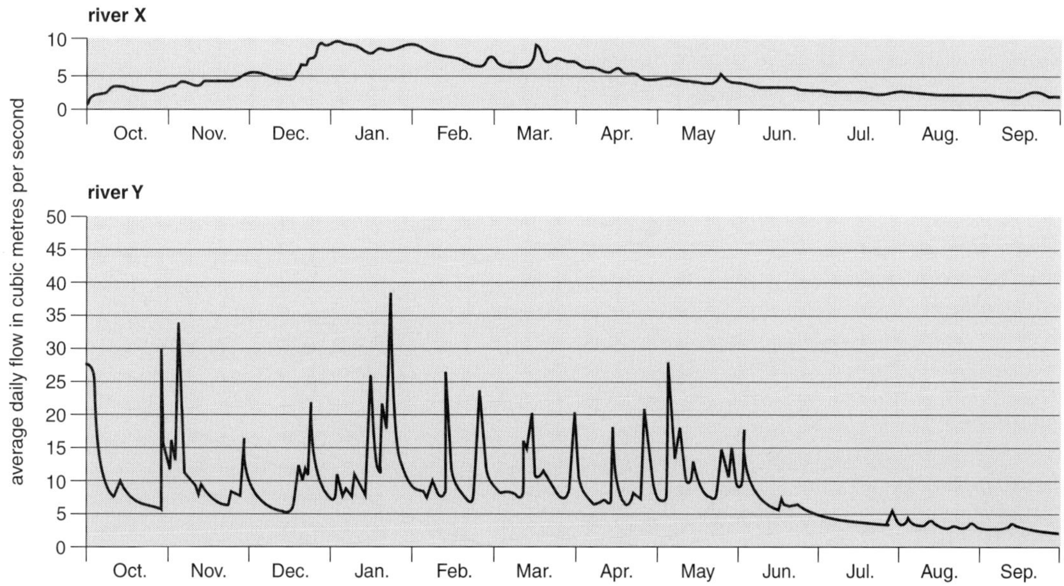

Figure 2.2A The flow of two rivers over a year

(b) Examine Figure 2.2B which shows the long profile of a river. Copy and complete the diagram by adding the following labels in the correct places:
deposition takes place here;
erosion takes place here;
some erosion and some deposition takes place here. (3)

(c) Study Figure 2.2C which shows a sketch of a floodplain.

i. Name the features labelled X, Y and Z Choose from: terrace, ox-bow lake and meander. (3)
ii. Outline the advantages and disadvantages of using this floodplain for farming. (4)

(d) Describe the conflicts which sometimes arise between different users of rivers. (4)

(20)

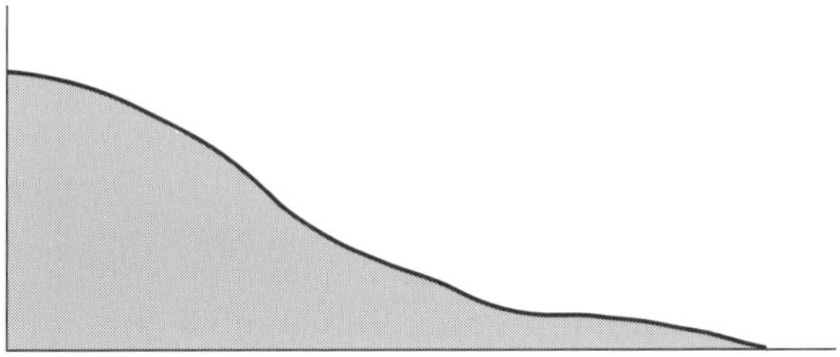
Figure 2.2B The long profile of a river

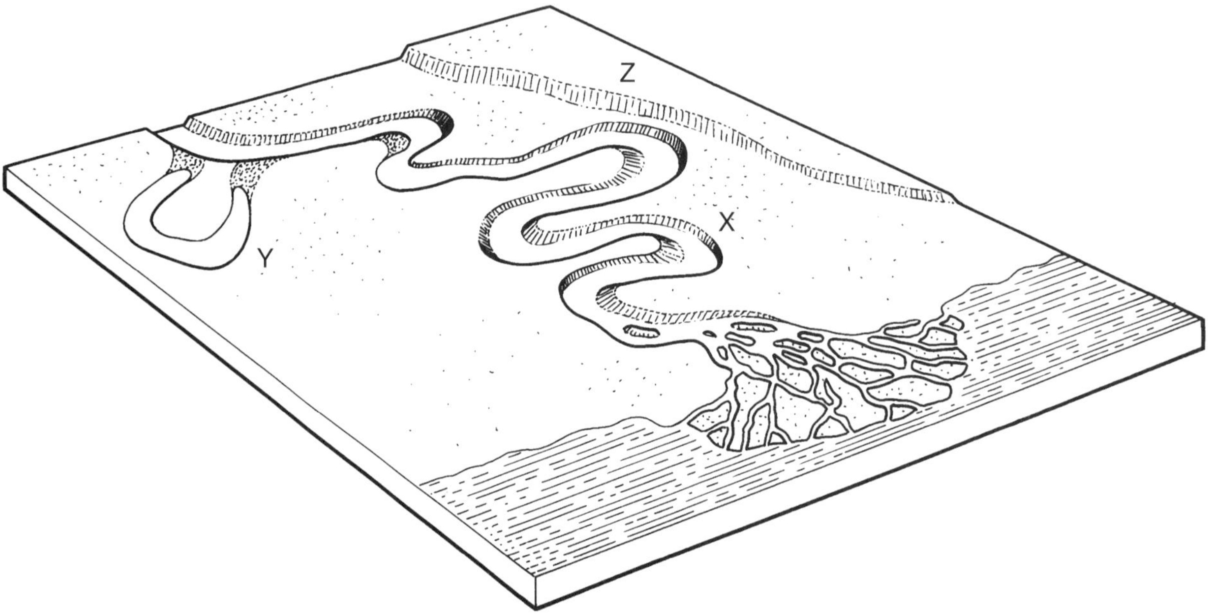

Figure 2.2C A floodplain

3 **(a)** Study the OS map on the inside front cover and then give the grid reference of:
   i. part of the floodplain of the Cuckmere River;
   ii. a meander on the Cuckmere River;
   iii. a small lake next the Cuckmere River;
   iv. the mouth of the Cuckmere River. (4)

(b) Look at Figure 2.3A which shows part of the course of a river. Copy the sketch and then add the following labels:
fast-moving water;
slow-moving water;
deposited material. (3)

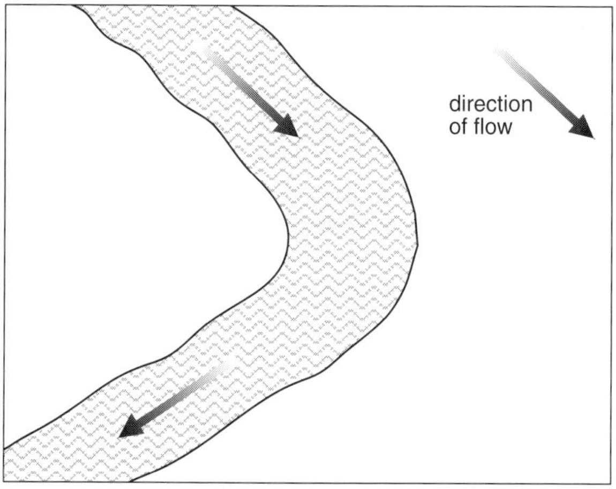

Figure 2.3A Part of the course of a river

(c) Examine the OS map on the inside front cover.
   i. Suggest ways in which the Cuckmere River and its valley is being used for leisure and tourism. (2)
   ii. Apart from leisure and tourism give one other way in which the Cuckmere River could be used by people. (1)

(d) Figure 2.3B shows some of the causes of flooding. What actions of people increase the risk of flooding in an area? (3)

(e) Examine Figure 2.3C which shows a dam across a river.
   i. Give two reasons why dams are sometimes built across rivers. (3)

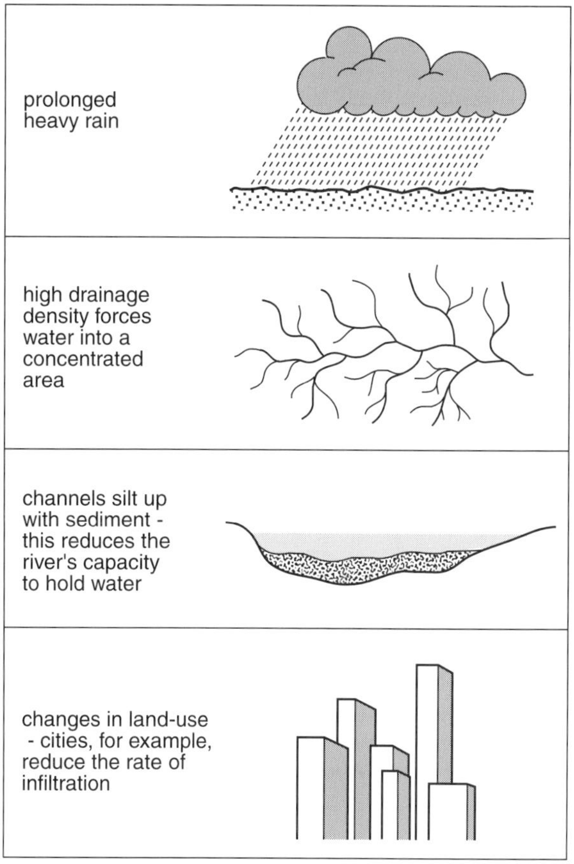

Figure 2.3B Some of the causes of flooding

   ii. Give one effect of a dam on the flow of a river. (1)
   iii. Explain why some people are against damming rivers. (3)

(20)

Figure 2.3C A dam across a river

EXTENSION QUESTIONS

4 (a) Examine the flow of the Cuckmere River on the OS map on the inside front cover.

i. Describe the physical features of the Cuckmere River on its course from 521020 to 516977. (4)

ii. Figure 2.4A shows the Cuckmere River from the viewpoint at 511009. Use an annotated sketch to help you describe and explain the flow of water at this point. (6)

Figure 2.4A The Cuckmere River

iii. Using map evidence suggest possible conflicts which might arise over the use of the Cuckmere River. (5)

(b) Figure 2.4B shows a model of a river basin while Figure 2.4C shows a cross-section of the river at X.

i. Draw two more cross-sections to show the river valley at Y and Z. (2)

ii. Describe and explain the different processes which shape the upper and lower courses of rivers. (6)

iii. State two river features which are often found in the upper courses of rivers and two river features which are often found in the lower courses of rivers. (2)

(25)

Figure 2.4C A cross-section of a river

5 (a) Examine Figure 2.5A which shows the regime of a river. Describe and explain the regime of this river. (4)

(b) Study Figure 2.5B which shows the drainage basin of the River Lyn when it experienced major flooding in 1952.

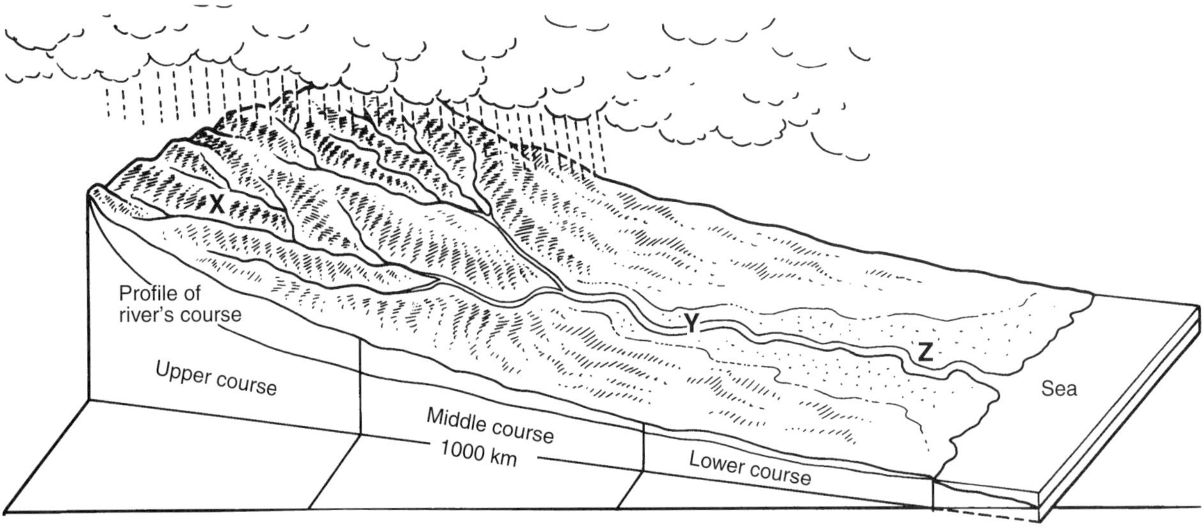

Figure 2.4B A model of a river basin

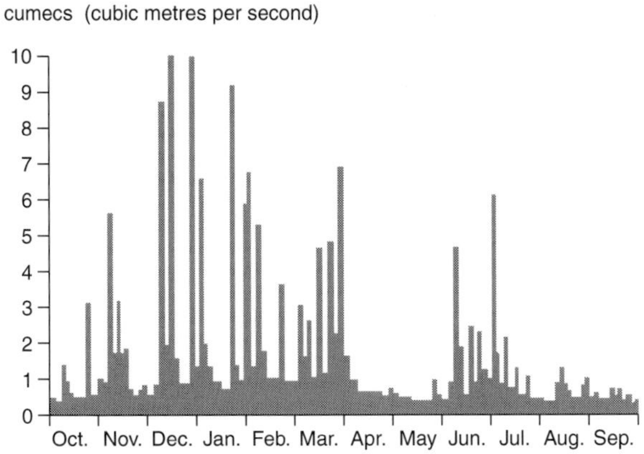

Figure 2.5A The regime of a river

i. Discuss the physical causes of the Lyn Flood. (2)
ii. Outline ways in which people may have contributed to the flooding. (2)
iii. Suggest measures which would help to prevent future flooding in this area. (3)

(c) Cities have an effect on surface infiltration.
i. Give the meaning of the term 'surface infiltration'. (2)
ii. Describe and explain how building cities next to rivers can affect surface infiltration. (2)

(d) Draw a cross-section sketch of the flood plain of a river to show the following features:
i. levees; (2)
ii. terraces; (2)
iii. alluvium. (2)

(e) Draw a sketch to help you describe how an ox-bow lake is formed. (4)

(25)

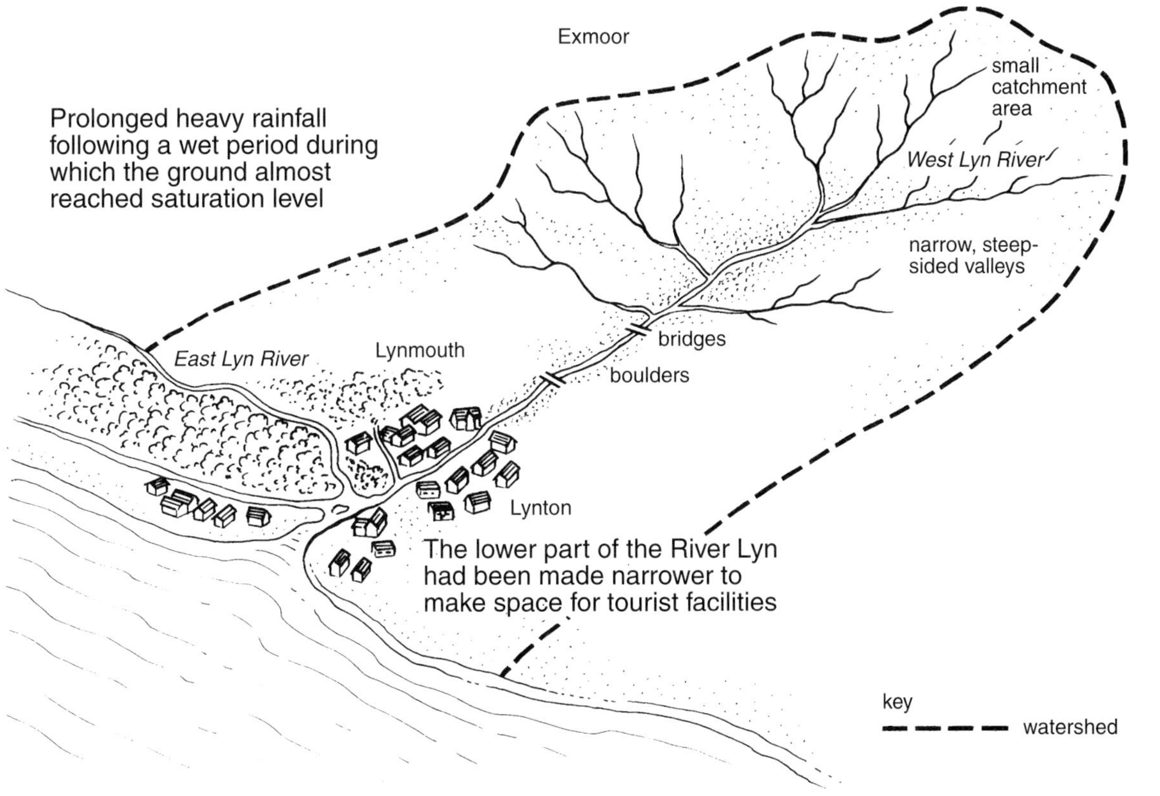

Figure 2.5B The drainage basin of the River Lyn

6 (a) Look at Figure 2.6A which shows a river.

i. Describe ways in which a river erodes its banks. (4)

ii. Describe ways in which a river transports its load. (3)

iii. Explain why a river deposits its load. (2)

(b) Figure 2.6B shows a waterfall.
Draw a labelled diagram to show one way in which waterfalls are formed. (4)

Figure 2.6A A river

(c) Outline the effects which each of the following will have on river flow and water quality in a river system:

i. water storage reservoir; (3)

ii. industrial developments. (3)

(d) Figure 2.6C shows the results of a river survey.
Describe and explain this data. (6)

(25)

Figure 2.6B A waterfall

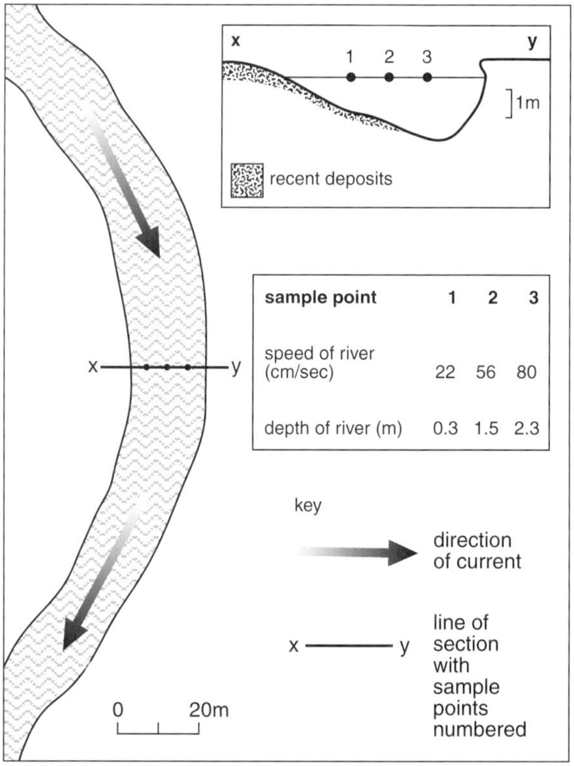

Figure 2.6C The results of a river survey

3 Coasts

Key words

abrasion a form of erosion which involves sand and rock fragments, which are being carried by the sea, scraping and grinding away at cliffs and other rock surfaces

arch a hole, formed by wave erosion, which extends all the way through a headland

attrition (also known as corrasion) a process of erosion in which particles are rounded and gradually reduced in size by repeatedly being struck against one another

backwash water returning from the beach to the sea

bar deposits of sand and shingle which sometimes extend across a bay or estuary

bay a wide, curving indentation in the coastline

beach an accumulation of sand, shingle or pebbles which has been deposited by waves at the edge of the sea

blowhole a hole, formed by erosion, at the top of a cliff

cave a hollow, formed by erosion, in the side of a cliff

cliff a steep rock face next to the sea

coastline of deposition coastal areas with beaches, spits, bars and other landforms formed by material being deposited by the sea

coastline of erosion coastal areas with caves, arches, stacks and other landforms formed by wave erosion

constructive waves low, gentle waves which have a constructive effect on the shoreline; constructive waves build up steep beaches because the swash is more powerful than the backwash

destructive waves waves which have a destructive effect on the shoreline; destructive waves remove sand and shingle from beaches because the backwash is more powerful than the swash

estuary the wide mouth of a river which is affected by sea tides

fetch the distance a wave travels before it reaches the land; longer fetches usually mean larger and more powerful waves

groynes wooden or concrete barriers which have been built at right angles to the beach to prevent the removal of sand and shingle by longshore drift

headland an area of higher ground jutting out into the sea

hydraulic action a process of erosion which involves cliffs and other shoreline rocks being loosened by the sheer force of waves

lagoon the area of shallow water which fills the space between a bar and the mainland

longshore drift the movement, by wave action, of sand and shingle along the coast

solution the dissolving of minerals within rocks such as limestone and chalk by sea water

spit a narrow bank of sand and shingle projecting out from a bend in the coast

stack a steep-sided rock-pillar surrounded by water

swash the water which moves up a beach

tombolo a beach that connects an island to the mainland; the island of Portland, in southern England, is connected to the coast by a tombolo

wave-cut platform a level or gently-sloping area of rocks at the base of a cliff

wave refraction the 'bending' of a wave as it reaches shallow water in its approach to the shore

CORE QUESTIONS

1 (a) Figure 3.1A shows a coastal area.
Name the coastal landforms labelled A, B, C, D, E and F.
Choose from: stack, cave, headland, blowhole, arch and cliff. (3)

(b) Describe how any *two* of the features labelled A, B, C, D, E and F in Figure 3.1A were formed. (6)

(c) Figure 3.1B shows a photograph of a coastal area.

i. Describe two physical features of this coastal area which make it suitable for tourism. (4)

ii. Outline ways in which tourist activities have changed this coastal area. (2)

iii. Describe how the sea moves sand and pebbles along the coast. (3)

(d) Figure 3.1C shows a beach on the North Sea coast.

i. What is the name of the wooden structures which have been built on this beach? (1)

ii. Explain why these structures have been built. (1)

(20)

Figure 3.1B A coastal area

Figure 3.1C A beach on the North Sea coast

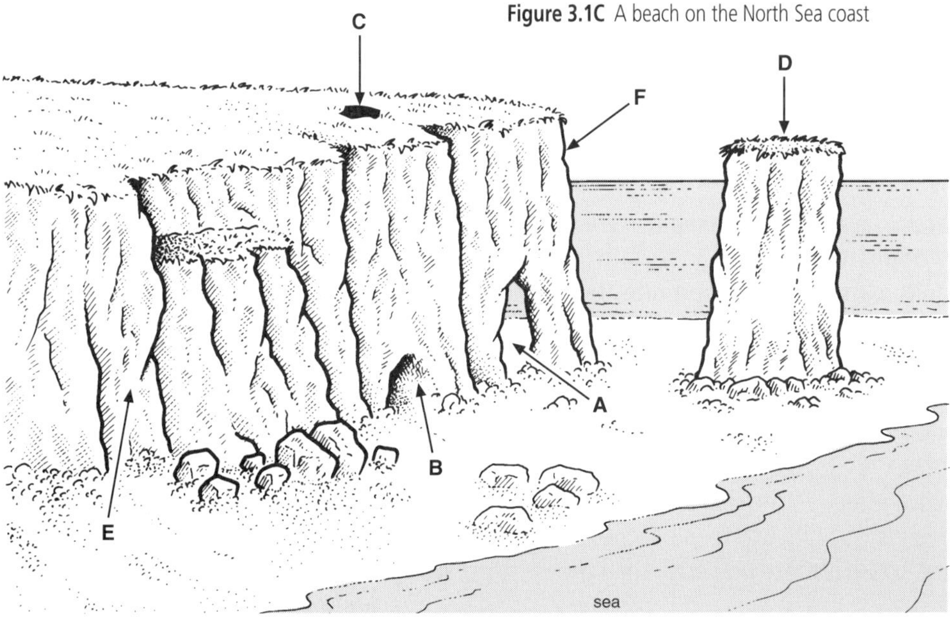

Figure 3.1A A coastal area

2 (a) Examine Figure 3.2A which shows the Isle of Purbeck in southern England.

i. Copy the sketch and then label the following features:
soft rock
hard rock
headland
bay (2)

ii. Which of the places (X, Y or Z) would provide the best location for a coastal resort? Give three reasons for your choice. (4)

(b) Study Figures 3.2B and 3.2C which show two different parts of the coast at Dorset in the south of England.

i. Is Figure 3.2B a coastline of erosion or a coastline of deposition? Give reasons for your answer. (4)

ii. Is Figure 3.2C a coastline of erosion or a coastline of deposition? Give reasons for your answer. (4)

(c) Figure 3.2D shows a new boat marina while Figure 3.2E shows two newspaper headlines about new marinas.
State the effect a new marina will have on:

i. the appearance of the coast; (2)
ii. birds and plants in the coastal area; (2)
iii. the land next to the marina. (2)

(20)

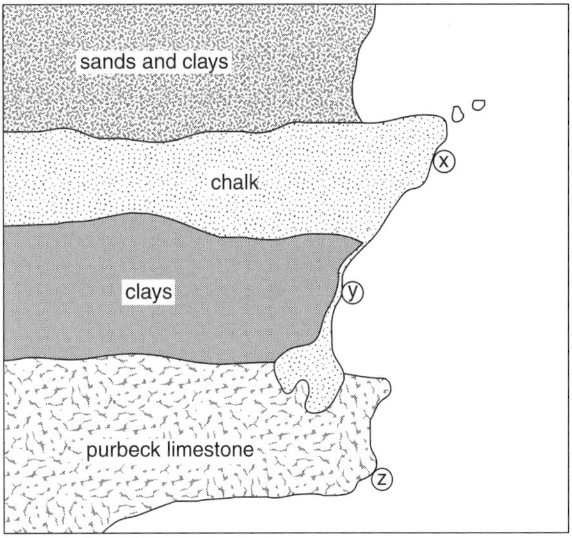

Figure 3.2A The Isle of Purbeck

Figure 3.2B Part of the coast at Dorset

Figure 3.2C Part of the coast at Dorset

Figure 3.2D A new boat marina

WILDLIFE GROUPS OPPOSE PLANS FOR 'MEGA-MARINA'

TWO HUNDRED NEW MARINAS PLANNED FOR THE ENGLISH COAST

Figure 3.2E Newspaper headlines about new marinas

EXTENSION QUESTIONS

3 (a) Describe the section of the Sussex coastline shown on the OS map on the inside front cover. (5)

(b) Examine the coastal area on the map on the inside front cover.

i. State one danger which this coastal area presents for people and one danger which this coastal area presents for shipping. (2)

ii. What has or could be done to make this coastal area safer for people and shipping? (2)

(c) Figure 3.3A shows the coastguard houses at the Birling Gap on the Sussex coast while Figure 3.3B shows part of a newspaper article about the houses.

i. Account for the coastal erosion which is taking place in this part of the Sussex coast. (4)

ii. What measures could be taken to protect the coastline from further erosion? (4)

iii. Outline one reason why some people might be against these measures. (2)

(d) Examine Figure 3.3C which shows the cliffs at Beachy Head.
Outline the importance of rock type in the formation of cliffs such as those at Beachy Head. (2)

(e) Figure 3.3D shows a pebble on the beach on the Sussex coast. Name and describe the processes which have affected this pebble. (4)

(25)

The coastguard houses at the Birling Gap on the Sussex Coast are about to fall into the sea according to a leading expert on cliff-erosion. 'The cliffs are retreating at a rate of a centimetre a year' the expert stated. 'It is only a matter of time before the houses, which are less than 20 metres from the edge of the cliff, will become too dangerous for people to live in.'

Figure 3.3B Part of a newspaper article

Figure 3.3A Coastguard houses at Birling Gap

Figure 3.3C The cliffs at Beachy Head

Figure 3.3D A pebble on the beach on the Sussex coast

Figure 3.4A Waves arriving at the coast of eastern Britain

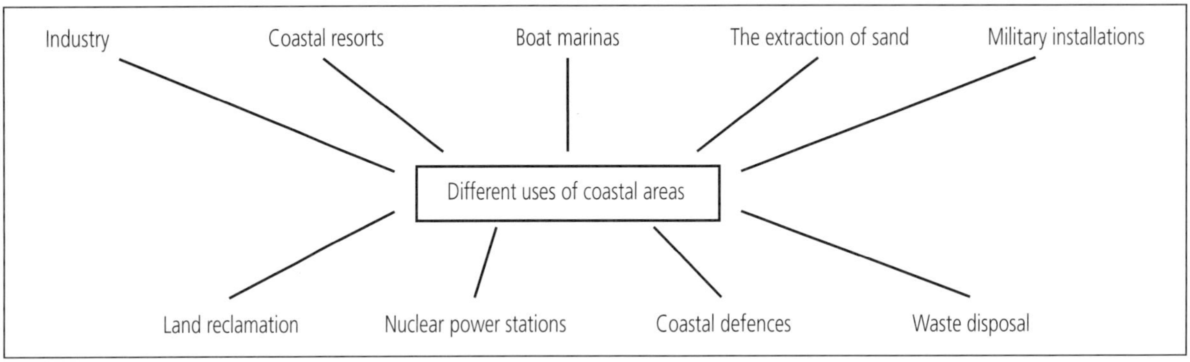

Figure 3.4B Different uses of coastal areas

4 **(a)** Figure 3.4A shows waves arriving at the coast of eastern Britain. Describe and explain the different ways in which waves shape the coast. (6)

(b) Study Figure 3.4B which shows different uses of coastal areas.

i. For any *two* of these uses outline the advantages of a location next to the coast. (4)

ii. For any *two* of these uses outline the effect they have on the coastal environment. (4)

(c) Examine Figure 3.4C which shows a section of coast which has been protected.

i. State two ways in which this coast is being protected. (2)

ii. Explain why it was necessary to take these measures. (3)

iii. Discuss one type of conflict which sometimes arises from the construction of coastal protection schemes. (2)

(d) 'Both human and physical factors are combining to destroy coastal areas.'
Use named examples to help you discuss the accuracy of this statement. (4)

(25)

Figure 3.4C A section of protected coastline

TOPICS

4

Special Landscapes

Key words

abrasion the erosion which occurs when a glacier carrying rocks and stones wears away the rocks it passes over

arête a knife-edge ridge between two corries

carbonation a form of chemical weathering which involves acid, formed by the solution of atmospheric carbon dioxide in water, dissolving rocks such as limestone

carboniferous limestone scenery scenery made up of limestone pavements, sink-holes, caverns, limestone pillars and limestone scars

chemical weathering the breakdown, but not removal, of rocks by chemical processes such as carbonation

clints the blocks of limestone which, along with grikes (the joints), make up limestone pavements

corrie a large circular hollow which has been eroded, by ice, in a glaciated mountain area

crevasses vertical cracks in ice which form when the ice moves over steeper land

dry valley a valley, usually in chalk or carboniferous limestone landscapes, which has no permanent river or stream

erosion the various ways in which rock is worn away by ice, water and wind

freeze-thaw action the action of water when it repeatedly freezes and thaws inside rocks; scree is an example of a landform produced by freeze-thaw action

grikes the joints, between the clints (the blocks of limestone), on limestone pavements

hanging valley a smaller side valley, hanging over a larger valley, in a glaciated upland area

honeypot a location which is particularly popular with visitors and tourists; planners often develop a number of honeypot sites in national parks so that other parts of the park will remain quieter and unspoilt

impermeable rocks rocks which do not allow the passage of water

limestone pavement a bare limestone surface made up of blocks (clints) and joints (grikes)

limestone pillar a pillar of limestone formed when a stalactite joins a stalagmite to create a continuous column

mechanical weathering the wearing down, but not removal, of rock without chemical change taking place

national park an area of scenic or special interest which is protected by a series of rules and laws

permeable rocks rocks which water can pass through

plucking a form of erosion which involves the removal of loose rock by glaciers

pyramidal peak a sharp peak formed when three or more corries have cut into the top of a mountain

scree broken rocks which have fallen away, often because of freeze-thaw action, from the side of a hill or mountain

stalactite a column of limestone hanging from the roof of a limestone cave

stalagmite a column of limestone formed upwards from the floor of a limestone cave

U-shaped valley a glaciated valley formed after ice deepened and widened a smaller and narrower V-shaped valley

weathering the breakdown of rocks by the action of rain, frost, wind and other elements of the weather or by plants and animals; weathering differs from erosion in that no movement of the broken-down material takes place

CORE QUESTIONS

1 **(a)** Examine Figure 4.1A which shows a glaciated upland region. Name the landforms labelled 1 to 6.
Choose from: hanging valley, corrie, arête, pyramidal peak, U-shaped valley and truncated spur. (3)

(b) Figure 4.1B shows how one of the landforms in Figure 4.1A was formed.
i. Name the landform being formed in Figure 4.1B. (1)
ii. Copy and complete the sketch by labelling the following features:
ice plucking at the backwall;
ice with greater erosive power;
crevasse. (3)

(c) Look at Figure 4.1C which shows part of the Lake District – an upland glaciated region in north west England which attracts many visitors.
i. Give three reasons why this area attracts so many visitors. (3)
ii. Apart from tourism and leisure give three other ways this landscape can be used by people. (3)

(d) Outline the problems which large numbers of visitors create for upland areas such as the Lake District. (4)

(e) What steps can be taken to protect beautiful landscapes such as the Lake District? (3)

(20)

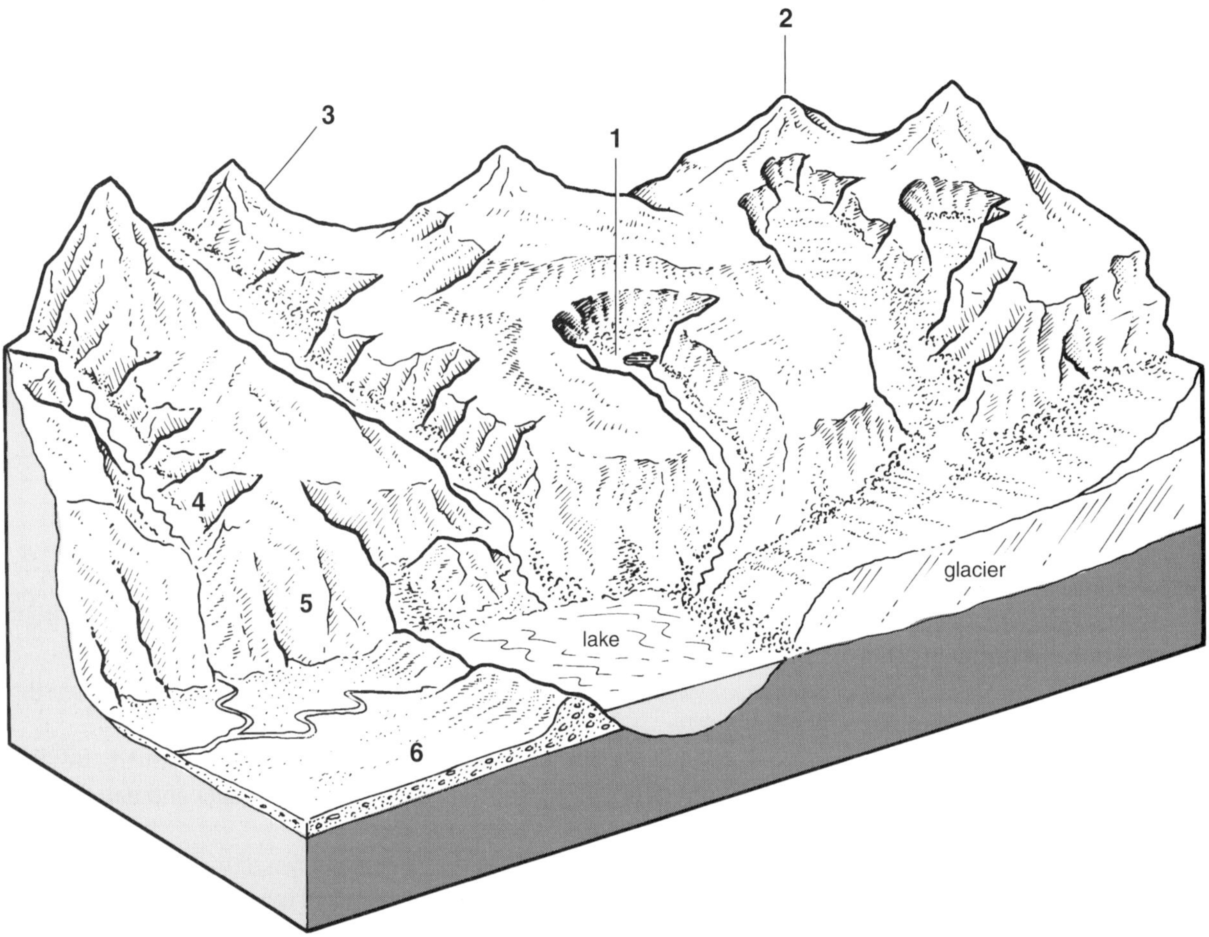

Figure 4.1A A glaciated upland region

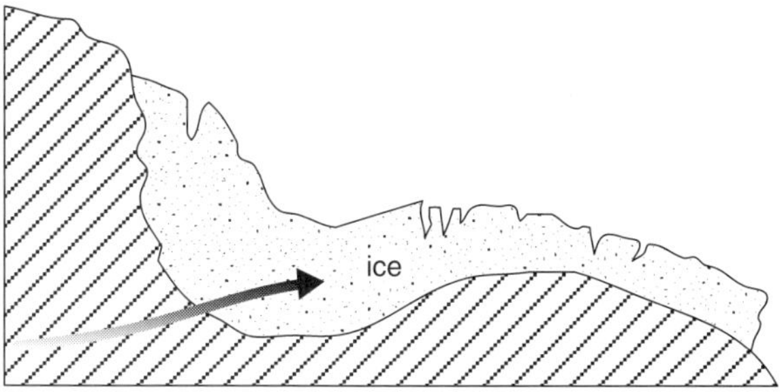

Figure 4.1B The formation of a landform

Figure 4.1C Part of the Lake District

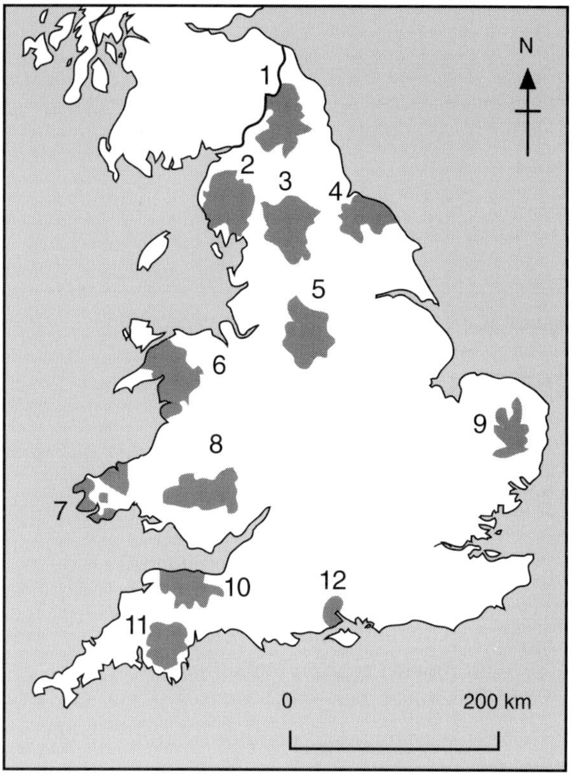

Figure 4.2A The national parks of England and Wales

2 (a) Figure 4.2A shows the national parks (numbered 1 to 12) of England and Wales. Name any two of these national parks. (2)

(b) Look at Figure 4.2B which shows part of a national park in England.

i. What sort of areas are made into national parks? Give examples. (3)

ii. Describe how national park rules will protect the area shown in the photograph. (3)

iii. What features of this area make it suitable for recreation and leisure? (3)

(c) 'Living and working in a national park is a mixed blessing.' State two ways in which national parks affect:

i. farmers; (2)

ii. visitors; (2)

iii. local residents. (2)

(d) Figure 4.2C shows users of land in the Lake District National Park. State three conflicts which might arise between these groups over the use of the land. (3)

(20)

Figure 4.2B Part of a national park in England

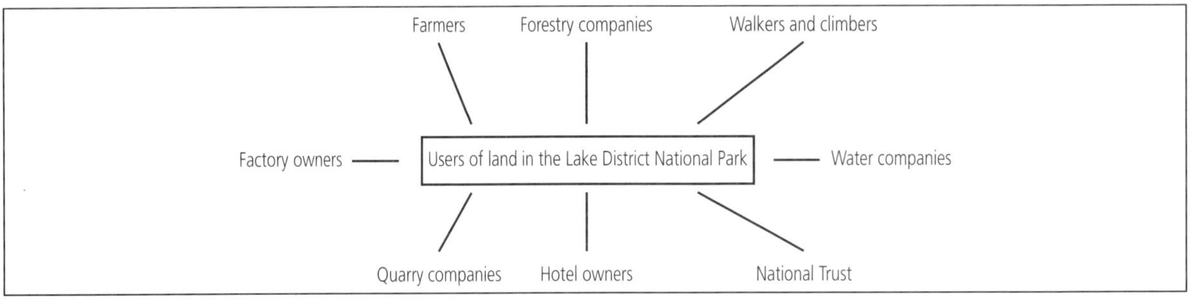

Figure 4.2C Users of land in the Lake District National Park

EXTENSION QUESTIONS

3 **(a)** Study Figure 4.3A which shows a glaciated trough in the Cairngorm Mountains of Scotland.

i. Draw a labelled sketch to identify the main features of this area and to explain how these features were formed. (6)

ii. Assess the usefulness of this area for human activities. (3)

iii. Who might object to the human activities you mentioned in your answer to (a)ii? (2)

(b) i. Account for the formation of the landscape feature shown in Figure 4.3B. (4)

ii. There is increasing pressure to use mountain areas for recreation and leisure.
What environmental problems may arise because of this? (5)

Figure 4.3B A landscape feature

(c) Examine Figure 4.3C which shows part of a tourist honeypot.

i. What is meant by the term 'tourist honeypot'? (2)

ii. Describe the attractions of a tourist honeypot you have studied. (3)

(25)

Figure 4.3A A glaciated trough in the Cairngorm mountains

Figure 4.3C A tourist 'honeypot'

4 **(a)** Examine Figure 4.4A which shows an area of carboniferous limestone. Describe and explain the landscape features associated with this type of area. (8)

(b) Figure 4.4B shows part of the Yorkshire Dales National Park while Figure 4.4C shows an extract from a tourist guide about the Yorkshire Dales.

i. Outline the economic opportunities presented by the landscape of the Yorkshire Dales. (2)

ii. Discuss the environmental conflicts which sometimes arise in areas, such as the Yorkshire Dales, which attract large numbers of visitors. (4)

(c) Look at Figure 4.4D which shows a farm in the Yorkshire Dales National Park. Discuss the benefits and problems experienced by farmers with farms in national park areas. (6)

(d) National parks are just one of the ways in which beautiful and important areas of countryside are protected.

i. Outline other ways in which beautiful and important areas of countryside are protected. (2)

ii. Give reasons why important areas of countryside are protected. (3)

(25)

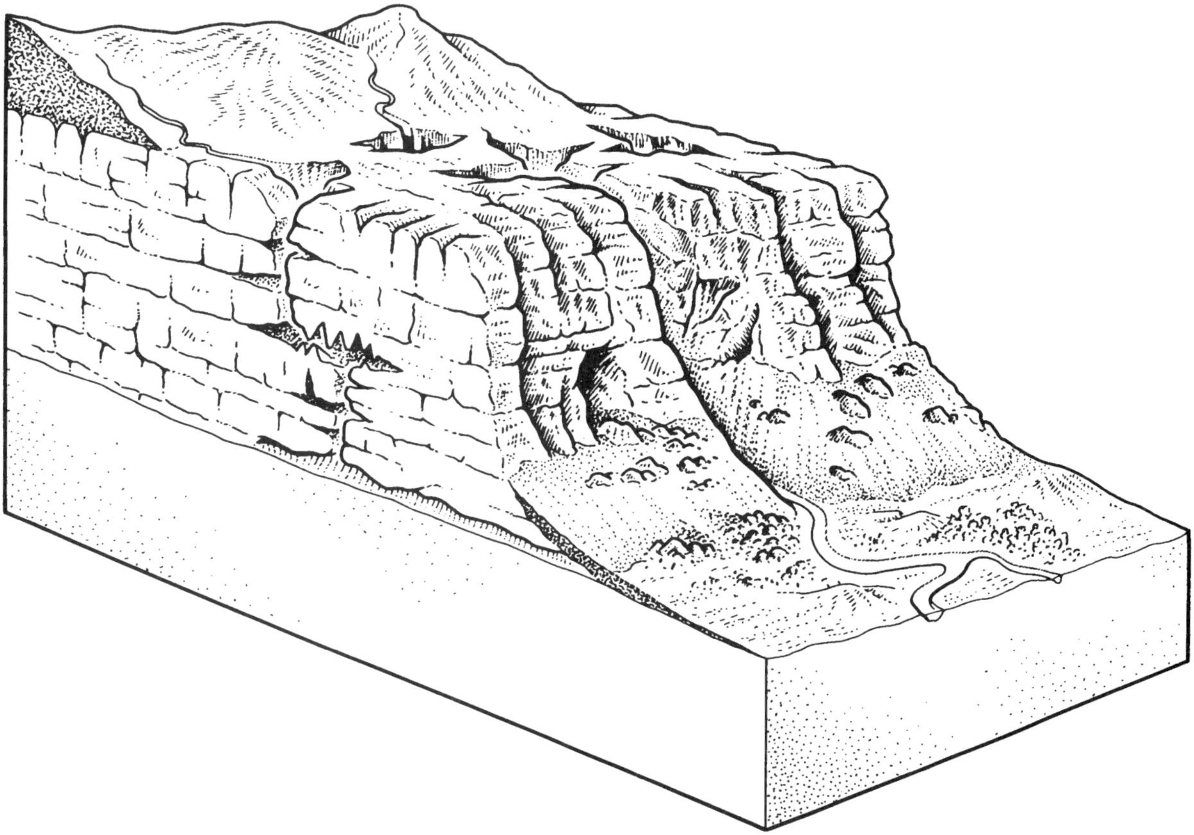

Figure 4.4A An area of Carboniferous limestone

Figure 4.4B Part of the Malham area of the Yorkshire Dales

The Yorkshire Dales offer some of the best walking areas in England. As well as the natural beauty of the area's limestone scenery the Yorkshire Dales also have the attraction of numerous sites of interest for the historian, geologist, cave-explorer and nature-lover. But if it is peace and quiet that you are looking for then it is best to avoid the area on Bank Holidays and Summer Sundays. . . .

Figure 4.4C An extract from a tourist guide about the Yorkshire Dales

Figure 4.4D A farm in the Yorkshire Dales National Park

TOPICS

5

Weather and Climate

Key words

air pressure the force exerted by air on the earth's surface
air stream a moving body of air
anemometer the instrument for measuring the speed of the wind
annual rainfall the total amount of rain a place receives in a year
anticyclone a high pressure system which brings settled weather
aspect the direction a slope faces
barometer the instrument for measuring air pressure
Beaufort Scale a scale for measuring the speed of the wind
climate a summary of average weather conditions based on figures collected and recorded over a period of 30 years or more
cold front the boundary between cold air and warm air
depression a low pressure system which brings unsettled weather
heat island the higher temperatures which occur in the centre of a city because of the heating from buildings and transport systems and by the release, at night, of heat which has accumulated in the city
isobar a line joining places with the same air pressure
micro climate the climate of a very small area
North Atlantic Drift a warm ocean current in the North Atlantic Ocean which helps to create milder conditions on the west side of the British Isles and Scandinavia
occluded front where a cold front overtakes a warm front
ocean current a movement of surface water which is warmer or colder than the surrounding water
Polar continental air cold and dry air which flows from the north over the land
Polar maritime air cold and wet air which flows from the north over the sea
rain gauge the instrument for measuring precipitation
rain shadow area an area of relatively low rainfall on the dry (lee) side of an upland area
range of temperature the difference between the highest and lowest temperatures experienced during a given period such as a day or a year
relief rain rain which occurs after moisture-laden air is forced to rise over high ground – as the air rises it cools causing water vapour to condense and rain to fall
Stevenson screen a wooden, white box on four legs which holds thermometers
sunshine recorder the instrument for measuring how long the sun has been shining
thermometer the instrument for measuring temperature
Tropical continental air warm and dry air which flows from the south over the land
Tropical maritime air warm and wet air which flows from the south over the sea
warm front the boundary between warm air and cold air
warm sector the wedge of warm air between a warm front and a cold front
weather the current condition of the atmosphere
weather satellite photographs photographs of weather systems sent back from satellites orbiting the Earth
wind vane the instrument for showing wind direction

CORE QUESTIONS

1 (a) Examine Figure 5.1A which shows a weather station.
Name any *four* of the weather instruments labelled A, B, C, D and E. Choose from: anemometer, soil thermometer, rain gauge, sunshine recorder and wind vane. (4)

(b) Name two elements of the weather which aren't measured by instruments. (2)

(c) Figure 5.1B shows a Stevenson Screen which is designed to hold thermometers.

i. Give one reason why thermometers are kept inside a Stevenson Screen. (1)

ii. Describe the appearance of the Stevenson Screen. (3)

iii. Explain the appearance of the Stevenson Screen. (3)

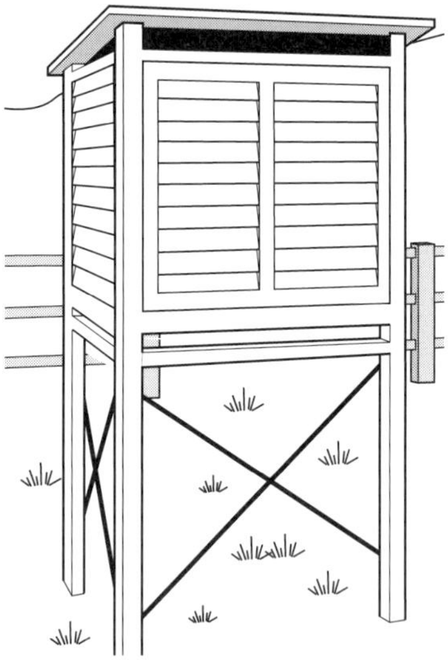

Figure 5.1B A Stevenson Screen

Figure 5.1A A weather station

(d) Give two reasons why weather stations are built on grass away from buildings. (2)

(e) Name two groups of people who make use of information from weather stations. (2)

(f) Study Figure 5.1C which shows three climate graphs. State which climate graph (X, Y or Z) has:

i. winter frosts;
ii. summer droughts;
iii. the smallest annual range of temperature. (3)

(20)

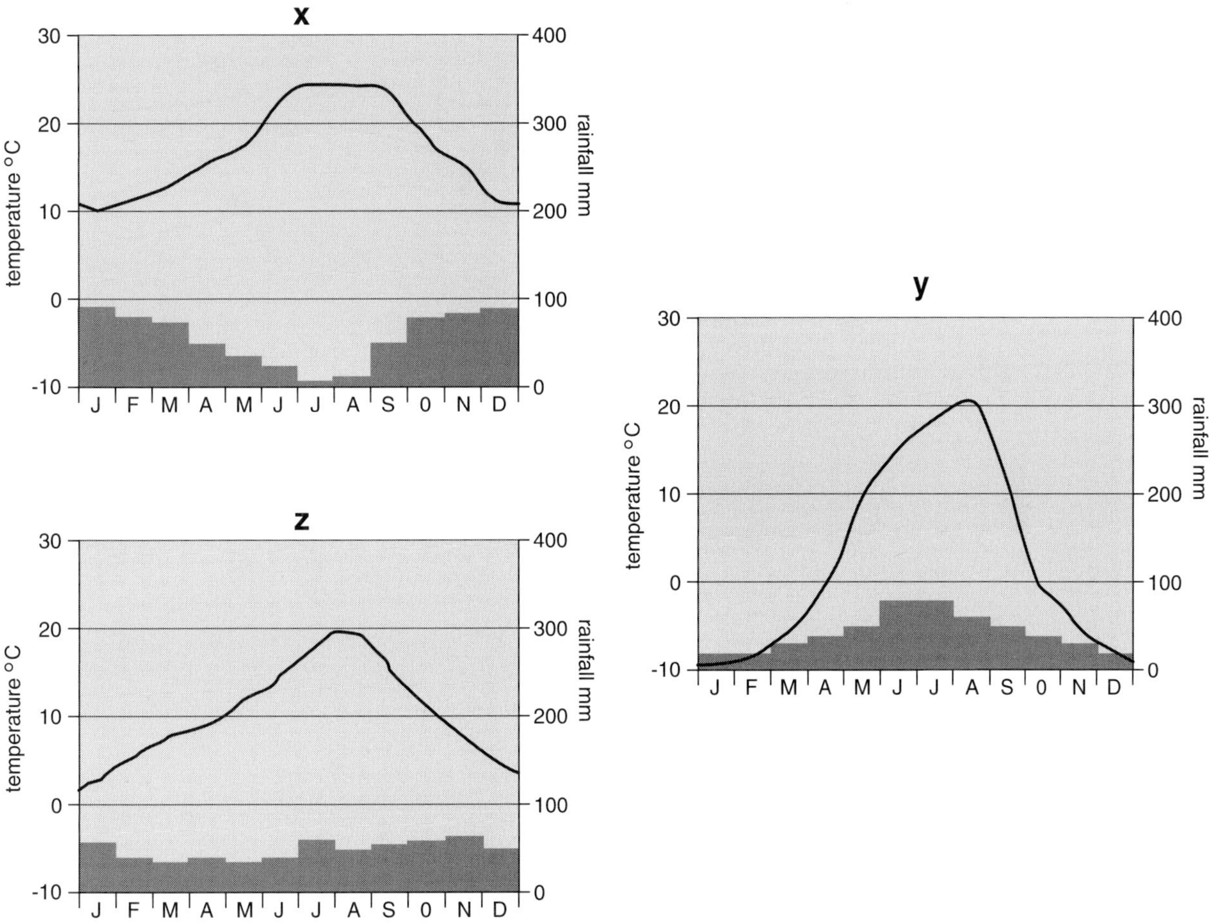

Figure 5.1C Three climate graphs

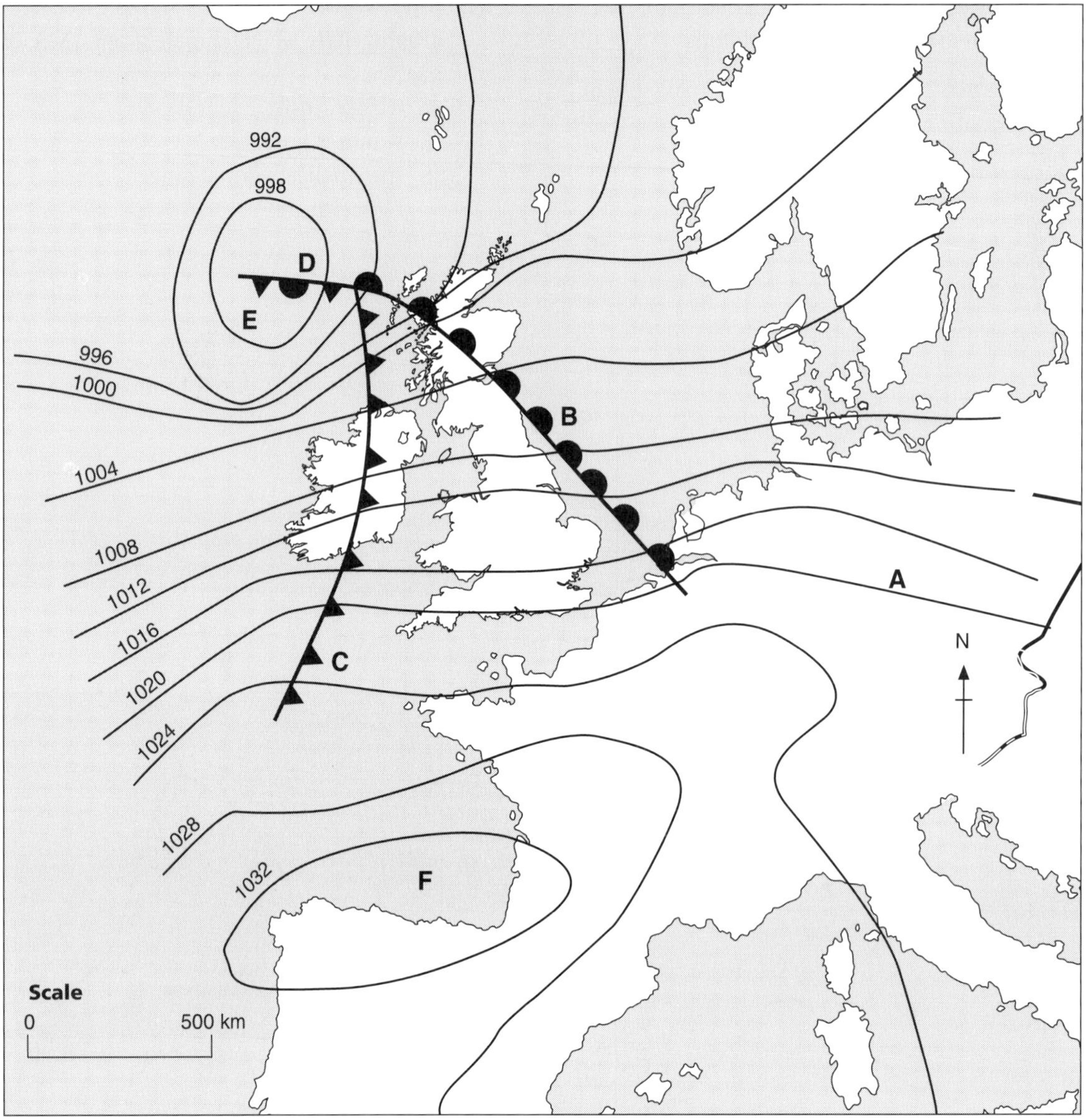

Figure 5.2A A weather chart

2 (a) Study Figure 5.2A which shows a weather chart. Name:

i. the lines marked with an A;
ii. the type of front at B;
iii. the type of front at C;
iv. the type of front at D;
v. the weather system at E;
vi. the weather system at F. (6)

(b) Examine Figure 5.2A.

i. Describe the weather conditions being experienced at E. (2)
ii. Describe the weather conditions being experienced at F. (2)
iii. Explain the weather conditions being experienced at F. (2)

(c) Figure 5.2B shows weather station symbols. State four things about the weather being experienced at this weather station. (4)

(d) Figure 5.2C shows relief rainfall.
Copy the sketch and then label the following:
rain-shadow area evaporation
condensation precipitation (4)

(20)

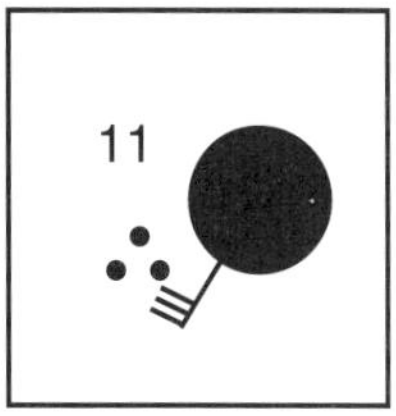

Figure 5.2B Weather station symbols

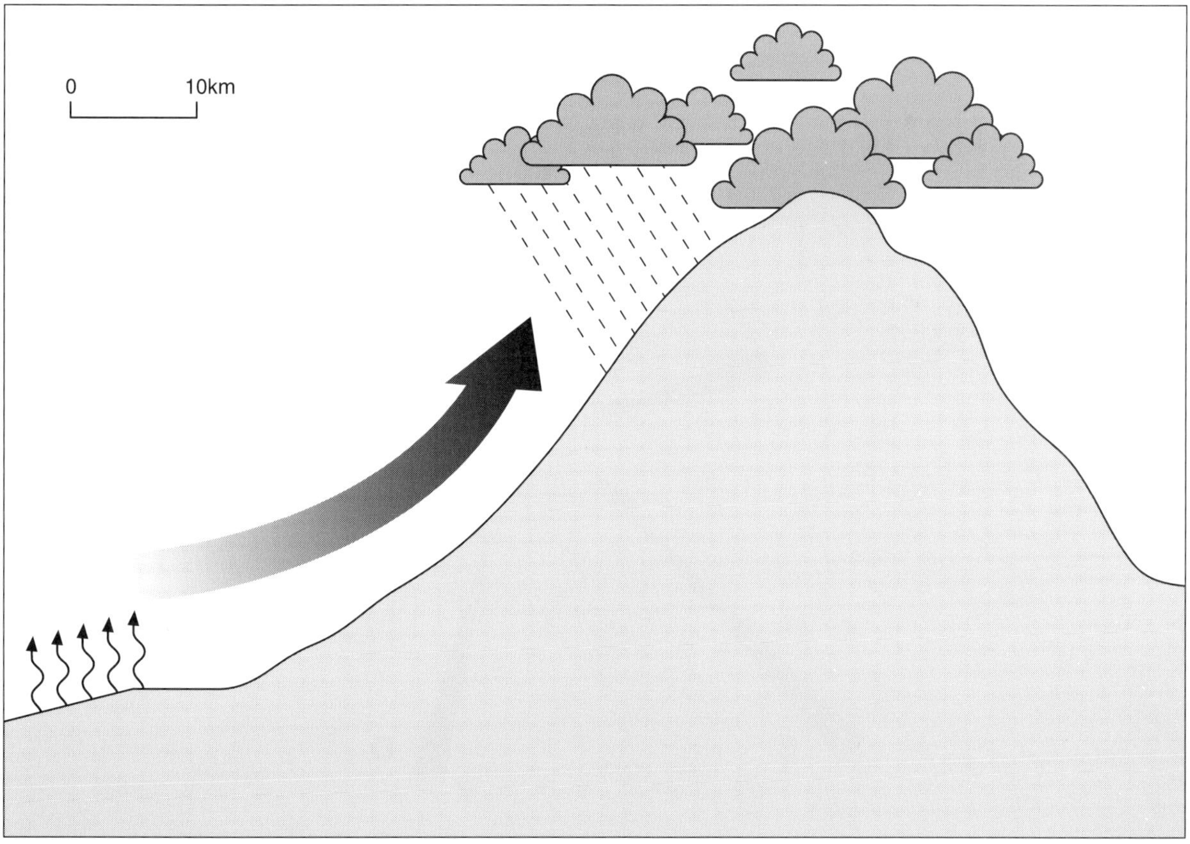

Figure 5.2C Relief rainfall

EXTENSION QUESTIONS

3 **(a)** Examine Figure 5.3A which shows the main air streams which affect the weather of the British Isles.

  i. Describe the effects of each of the air streams shown. (4)

  ii. Explain the effects of each of the air streams shown. (4)

(b) Describe how each of the following affects the climate of the British Isles:

  i. latitude; (1)

  ii. altitude; (1)

  iii. distance from sea; (1)

  iv. North Atlantic Drift; (1)

(c) Figure 5.3B is an extract from a magazine article about how cities affect the weather.

Explain why:

  i. temperatures are higher in cities than in nearby rural areas; (2)

  ii. wind speed is lower in cities than in nearby rural areas; (2)

  iii. visibility is poorer in cities than in nearby rural areas. (1)

> Researchers have calculated that Birmingham's city-centre receives 15 per cent less sunshine, 16 per cent more days of poor visibility and 20 per cent lower average wind speeds than the nearest rural areas. . . .

Figure 5.3B An extract from a magazine article

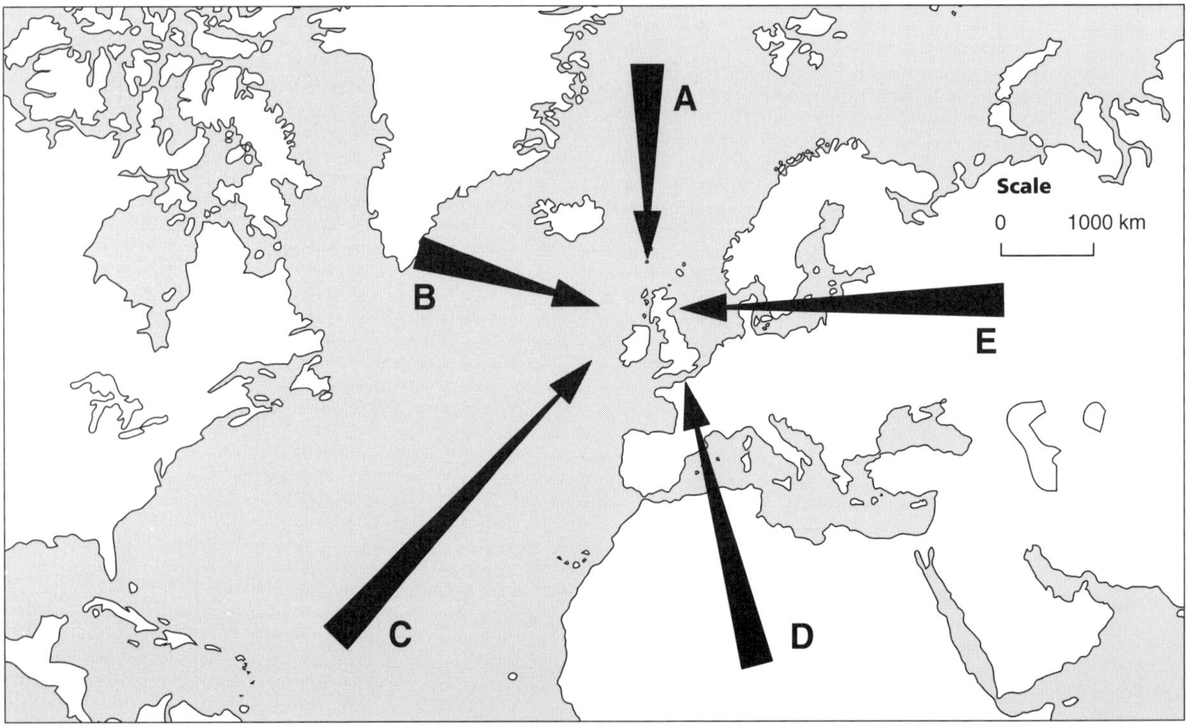

Figure 5.3A Air streams which affect the weather of the British Isles

(d) Examine Figure 5.3C which shows a weather chart for 21 June.

i. Describe and explain the weather conditions which are likely to be experienced at Glasgow over the following twenty-four hours. (4)

ii. Describe and explain the weather conditions which are likely to be experienced at Lyons over the following twenty-four hours. (4)

(25)

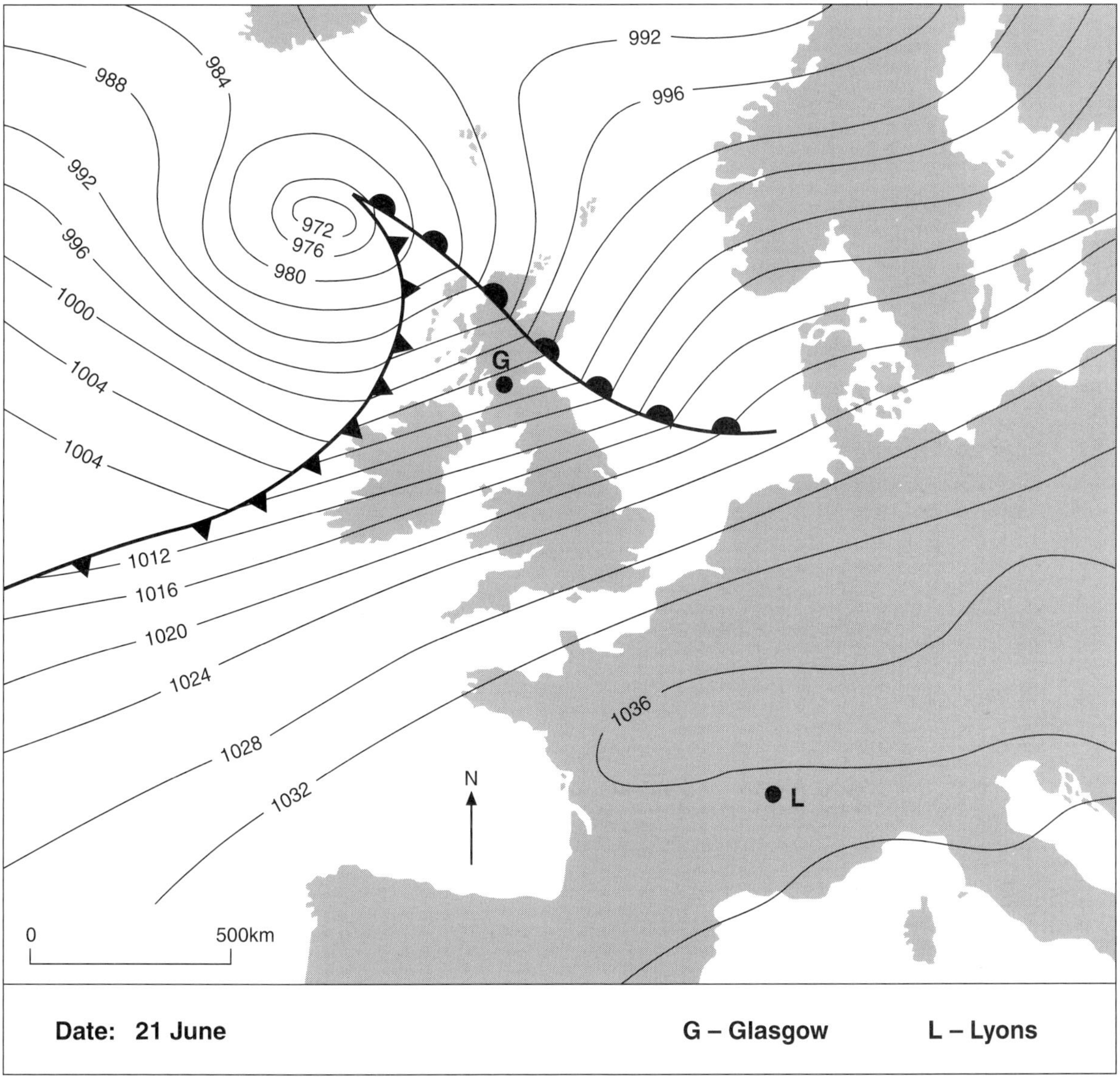

Figure 5.3C A weather chart for 21 June

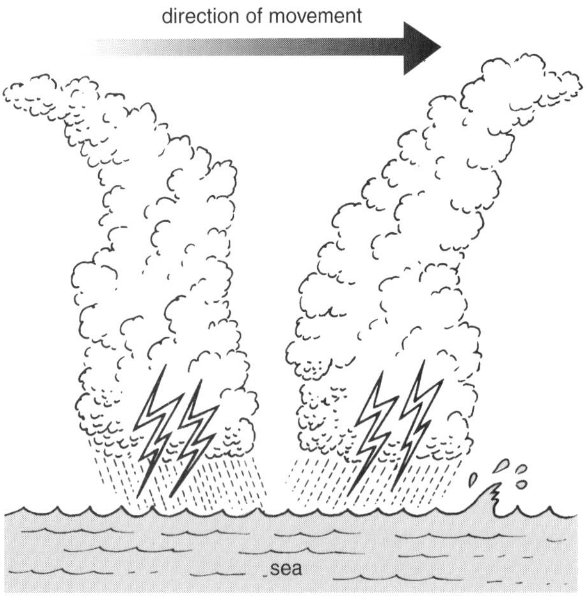

Figure 5.4A A cross-section of a tropical storm

4 (a) Examine Figure 5.4A which shows a cross-section of a tropical storm. Copy the sketch and then label the main features. (4)

(b) i. Name two countries affected by tropical storms. (1)

ii. Describe the distribution of tropical storm source areas. (3)

iii. Outline the dangers presented by tropical storms. (4)

iv. Discuss the measures which can be taken to try and reduce the impact of tropical storms. (3)

(c) Study Figure 5.4B which shows a landscape in south Asia – an area affected by tropical storms.
Outline ways in which the nature of this landscape will affect the impact of tropical storms. (5)

(d) Referring to named examples describe the effects of tropical storms on landscapes and their inhabitants. (5)

(25)

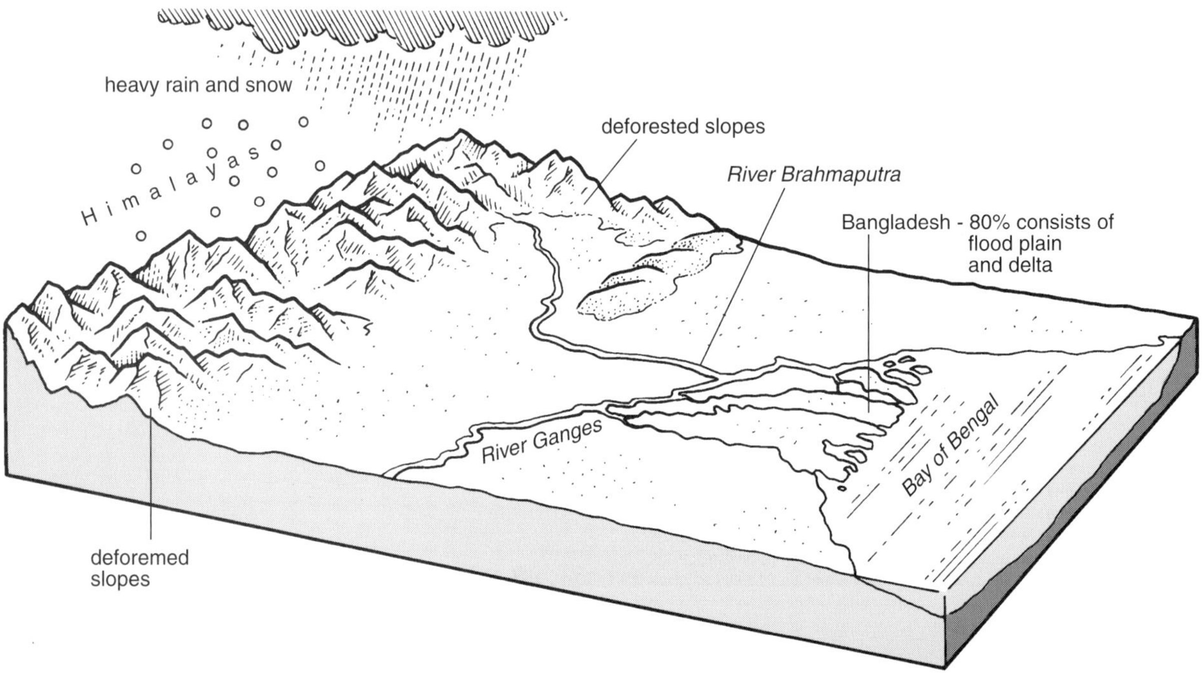

Figure 5.4B A landscape in south Asia

6 Settlement

Key words

central business district the centre of a city where you will find large department stores, offices, a city hall and a main railway station

commuter village a village next to a town or city; many people travel (commute) from the village to work in the city

conurbation a large built-up urban area formed when several cities and towns join together

counter-urbanisation the movement of people and employment away from larger towns and cities to smaller towns and villages

function the main purpose of a settlement, for example: a port, a market town or a route centre

gentrification the movement of richer people into a poorer part of a city where they change the area's social character

green belt an area of protected countryside around towns and cities

hinterland the area which is served by, for example, a port

inner-city the area around the central business district which often consists of a mixture of old housing and declining industries; the inner-city areas of major cities in economically developed countries are often being redeveloped to provide new housing and better living environments

market town a town, surrounded by good farmland, which provides services for farmers

millionaire city a city with more than a million inhabitants

new town a planned town, such as Crawley, which offers new housing and jobs

range of a service the maximum distance people will travel to make use of a service

relief road a road which has been built to reduce congestion on an existing road or roads

ring road a road which is built around a large settlement to reduce the number of vehicles entering the settlement

route centre a place where a number of different roads and railways meet

rural-urban fringe the land at the edge of a city where the city meets the countryside

self-help scheme a scheme which uses local people, and their skills, to improve conditions in an area

settlement a place where people live; settlements vary in size from single buildings to huge conurbations

shanty town an area of makeshift houses which has been built on waste ground usually at the edge of cities in economically developing countries

site the land on which a settlement has been built

situation the position of a settlement in relation to other places

sphere of influence the area which is served by a settlement or service

suburb a residential area in the outer part of a town or city

urban decay the deterioration of houses, factories, shops, etc.; urban decay is normally associated with the older parts of the inner-city

urban renewal (or regeneration) improving old and rundown parts of towns and cities

urban sprawl the outward spread of urban areas in an unplanned fashion

urban zone a distinct part of a town or city, for example: an industrial area, the central business district or a housing area

urbanisation the migration of rural populations into towns and cities

CORE QUESTIONS

1 (a) Study Figure 6.1A which shows the settlement hierarchy.

i. Name the type of settlement which has the largest population. (1)

ii. Describe the link between size of settlements and number of settlements. (1)

iii. Give two reasons why some settlements become large settlements while others remain small. (2)

iv. Give two types of services which are usually found in cities but not in villages. (2)

(b) i. Which of the following (A, B or C) is the correct meaning of the term 'sphere of influence':

A: the central part of a settlement;

B: the land on which the settlement has been built;

C: the area which uses the settlement's services? (1)

ii. State one way in which the sphere of influence of a village is different from the sphere of influence of a city. (1)

iii. Outline one way of finding out the sphere of influence of a settlement. (4)

(c) Figure 6.1B is part of a magazine article about changes in Singapore while Figure 6.1C shows new buildings next to the Singapore River.

i. Cities are continually changing. For a city you have studied describe two changes which have taken place. (4)

ii. For one of the changes you mentioned in your answer to (c)i. give two reasons why the change took place. (2)

iii. 'Urban change often has a major effect on people's lives.' Outline two ways in which urban change can affect peoples' lives. (2)

(20)

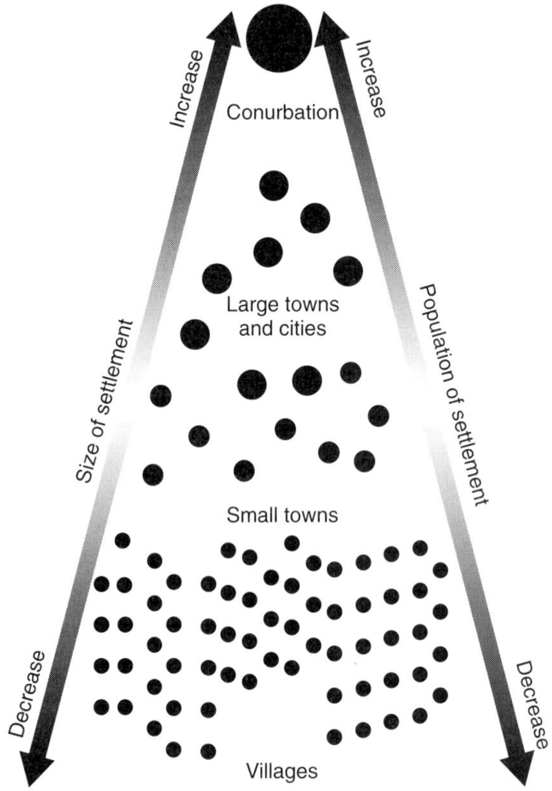

Figure 6.1A The settlement hierarchy

The city of Singapore is changing rapidly. Large areas of old housing are being cleared away to make way for new high-rise apartments, office-buildings and hotels. Thousands of families have already moved out of the overcrowded areas of substandard housing near the centre of Singapore to live in new flats on the outskirts of the city and in other parts of Singapore Island. At the same time the highly polluted and foul-smelling Singapore River is being cleaned up. New laws prevent farmers dumping waste into the river while the wooden bumboats which once lined the river front have been forced to move downriver. Old storage sheds and docking areas have been redeveloped to form a popular leisure and tourist area containing shops, restaurants and hotels.

Figure 6.1B Part of a magazine article

Figure 6.1C New buildings next to the Singapore River

2 For this question you should look at the OS map of the York area on the inside back cover.

(a) State four ways in which the land is being used in grid square 5956. (2)

(b) State one service which can be found in the village of Skelton (5656 and 5756). (1)

(c) Suggest the function of York. Choose from:
port mining centre tourist centre
Give two pieces of map evidence to support your choice. (3)

(d) State the grid reference of a square which has new housing. Give one reason for your choice of square. (2)

(e) Give two reasons why people living in the Holgate area (5851) might want to move to another part of the city. (2)

(f) Read the newspaper extract shown as Figure 6.2A.
Give the grid reference of a square on the map where a conflict may have arisen. State the reason for the conflict. (2)

(g) Examine the location of York Race Course (5949). Is this a good location for a race course? Give two reasons for your answer. (3)

> Battle lines are being drawn over the future use of the countryside around York. Road building, new housing, overhead transmission lines and outdoor recreation facilities are just some of the developments which have already caused conflict in the 'green belt' surrounding the city.

Figure 6.2A A newspaper extract

(h) Other than the race course, state one leisure activity, and its grid reference on the map, which is available for the people of York. (1)

(i) Figure 6.2B shows an area of 'green belt'.
i. What is a 'green belt'? (1)
ii. Give the grid reference of an area of 'green belt' around York. (1)
iii. 'The people of Skelton are against plans to build new houses on York's green belt.' Suggest two reasons why people in Skelton are against new houses being built on York's 'green belt'. (2)

(20)

Figure 6.2B An area of 'Green Belt'

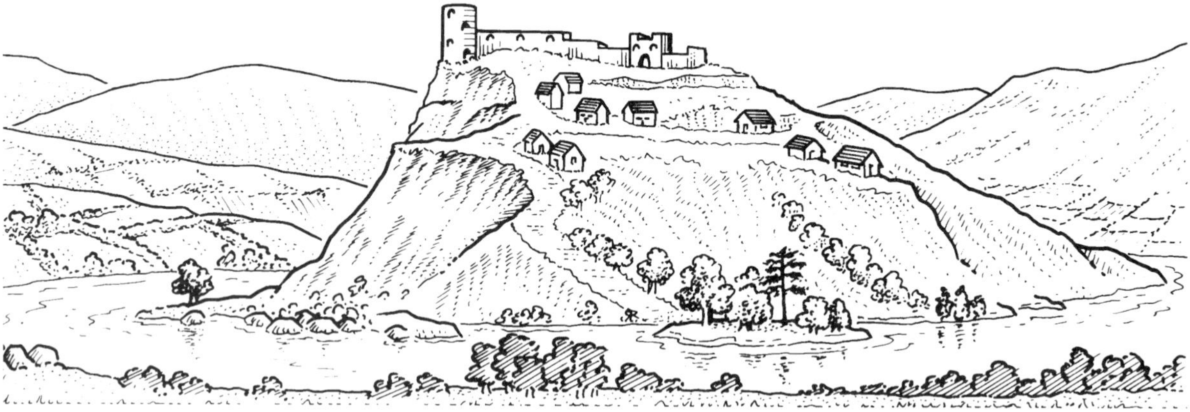

Figure 6.3A A settlement

3 (a) Look at Figure 6.3A which shows a settlement.

i. What evidence suggests that this settlement is an old settlement? (1)

ii. State two advantages of this site for the first people who settled there. (2)

iii. State two disadvantages of this site for the first people who settled there. (2)

iv. Why has this settlement not grown into a large settlement? (1)

(b) Figure 6.3B shows poor quality housing in an urban area.

i. Describe two housing problems in this area. (4)

ii. Suggest two ways in which housing in this area could be improved. (3)

iii. Poor quality housing is often found in the inner parts of cities. Explain why. (2)

(c) Study Figure 6.3C which shows the daily flow of traffic into a city.

i. Describe the flow of traffic into this city. (2)

ii. Give reasons for this pattern of traffic flow. (3)

(20)

Figure 6.3B Poor quality housing

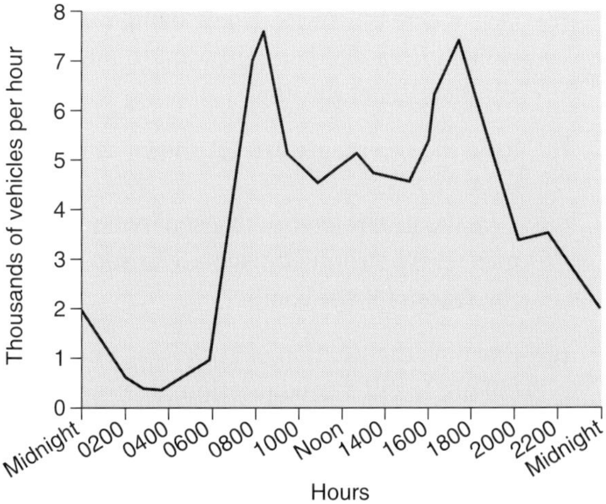

Figure 6.3C The daily flow of traffic into a city

4 (a) Examine Figure 6.4A which shows maps of five settlements.

i. Which map (A, B, C, D or E) shows a settlement with a linear shape? (1)

ii. Which map shows dispersed settlement? (1)

iii. Which map shows a nucleated settlement? (1)

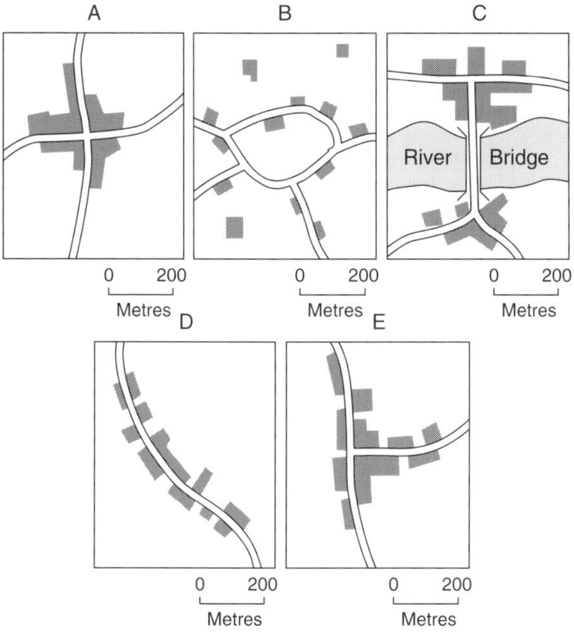

Figure 6.4A Five settlements

(b) Examine Figure 6.4B which shows an imaginary city.
Which part of the city (A, B, C, D or E) is most likely to have:

i. many shops and offices; (1)

ii. houses and factories mixed in together; (1)

iii. new houses; (1)

iv. port facilities; (1)

v. factories only? (1)

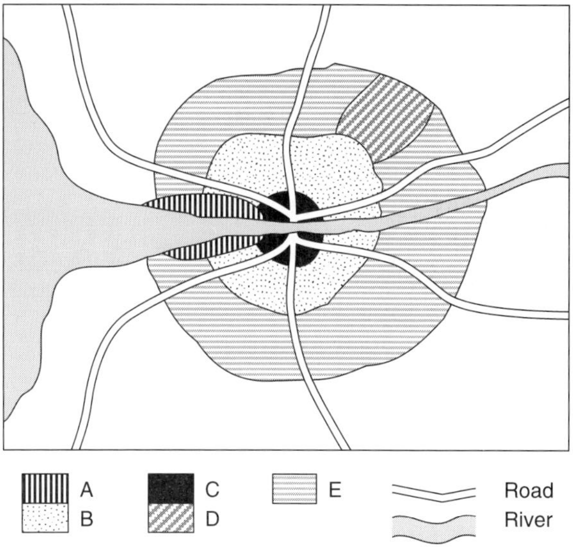

Figure 6.4B An imaginary city

(c) Study Figure 6.4C which shows problems in cities. For a city you have studied in an economically developed country describe one:

i. social problem; (2)

ii. economic problem; (2)

iii. environmental problem. (2)

(d) In the United Kingdom some people prefer to live near the centre of a city while others prefer to live in the suburbs.

i. Give two advantages of living near the centre of a city. (3)

ii. Give two advantages of living in the suburbs. (3)

(20)

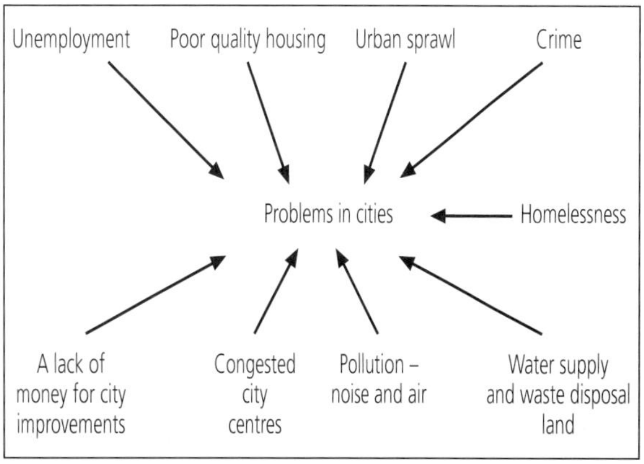

Figure 6.4C Problems in cities

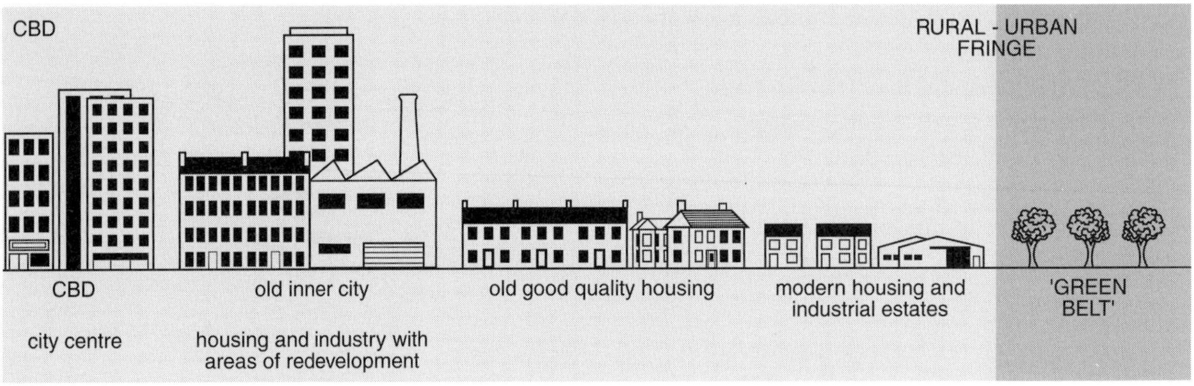

Figure 6.5A Land-use changes from the centre of a city to the rural-urban fringe

EXTENSION QUESTIONS

5 (a) Figure 6.5A shows how land-use changes from the centre of a city to the rural-urban fringe.

i. Describe the changes in land-use from the CBD to the rural-urban fringe. (3)

ii. Account for the changes in population density which occur between the CBD and the rural-urban fringe. (3)

(b) Examine Figure 6.5B which shows the central business district of a city in Europe.

i. Explain why tall buildings are a feature of central business districts. (2)

ii. Describe the different ways in which the land in central business districts is used. (3)

iii. 'The central business district is an area of land-use conflicts.'
Outline two land-use conflicts which exist in the central business district of a city you have studied. (3)

iv. For one of the conflicts mentioned in (b)iii. suggest how the conflict might be resolved. (2)

(c) Study Figure 6.5C which shows changes to a city.

i. Describe and explain three of the changes which have taken place. (6)

ii. Outline the problems which might arise with any one of these changes. (3)

(25)

Figure 6.5B The central business district of a city in Europe

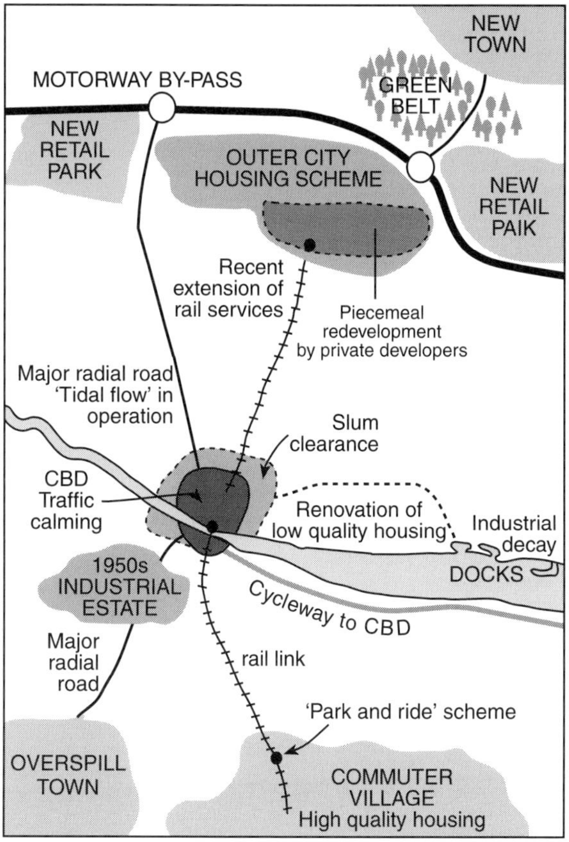

Figure 6.5C Changes to a city

6 For this question you should look at the OS map of York on the inside back cover.

(a) Describe the site of Skelton (5656 and 5756). (2)

(b) Identify the early site of York. State one advantage and one disadvantage of this site for early settlers. (2)

(c) Give a six-figure grid reference of a point on the map which falls within the central business district of York. State map evidence which supports your choice. (2)

(d) Suggest two reasons why no settlement has developed next to the river in grid square 5753. (2)

(e) York University has been built at 6250. Outline the advantages and disadvantages of this site for the university. (3)

(f) Figure 6.6A shows a model of a dormitory settlement.
State the meaning of the term 'dormitory settlement' and give two pieces of map evidence which suggest that Skelton is a dormitory settlement. (3)

(g) Compare and contrast the residential areas at Holgate (5851) and Chapel Fields (5651). (6)

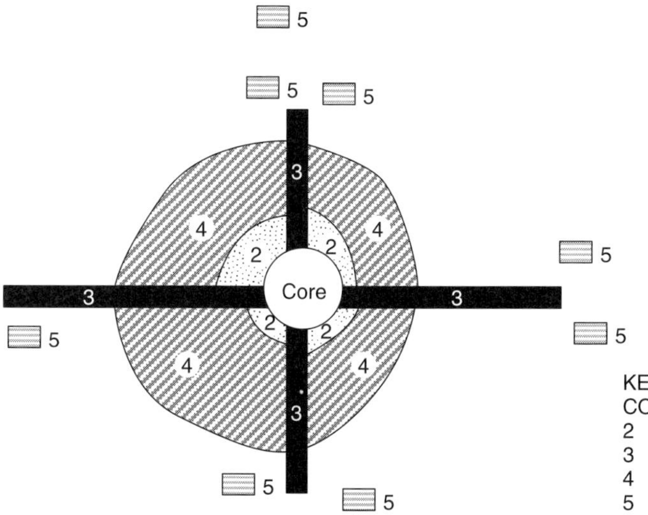

KEY
CORE developed before 1918 but with recent infilling
2 small areas of growth near village core 1918–1939
3 ribbon development 1930–1960
4 estates (private and council) mainly since 1950
5 gentrification of isolated properties

Figure 6.6A A model of a dormitory settlement

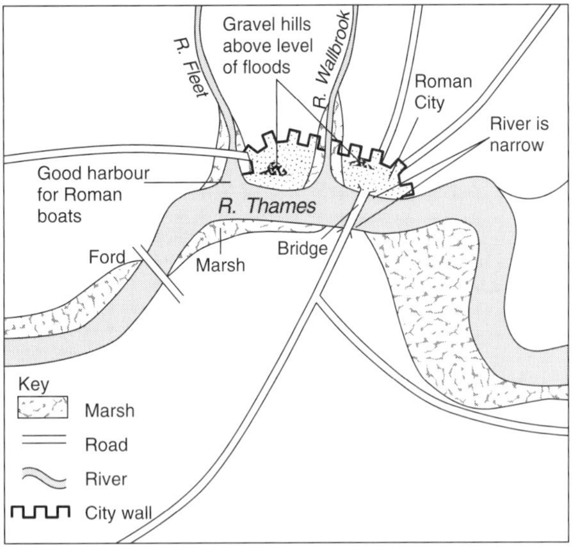

Figure 6.7A The original site of London

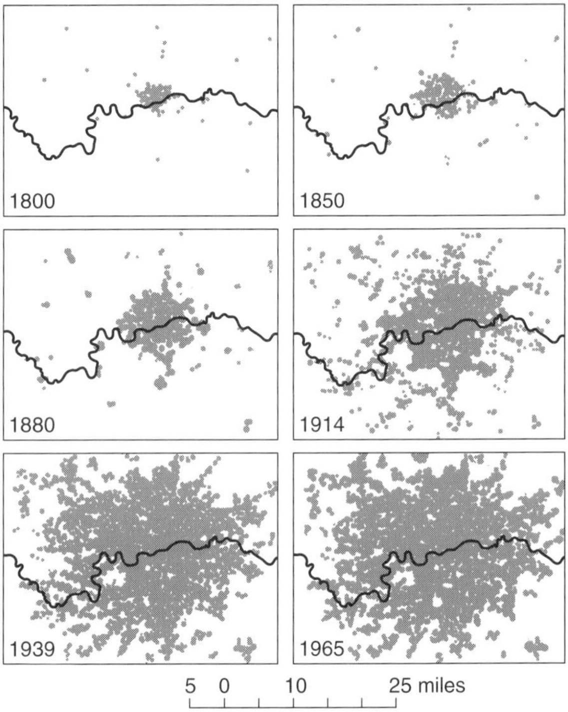

Figure 6.7B The growth of London

Figure 6.7C Part of the original site of London as it is today

7 (a) Figure 6.7A shows a map of the original site of London.

i. Why are the oldest parts of many settlements next to rivers? (3)

ii. Outline ways in which rivers helped the development of cities such as London. (3)

(b) Examine Figure 6.7B which shows the growth of London and Figure 6.7C which shows part of the original site of London as it is today.

i. 'The ancient core of London has been adapted to become the city's central business district.'
Suggest reasons why the central business districts of many cities develop around ancient cores. (3)

ii. State how Figure 6.7B shows the formation of a conurbation. (2)

iii. Why do some people object to the development of the countryside next to cities? (3)

(c) 'Redevelopment has greatly altered the urban landscape of London Docklands and changed the way of life of the people who live there.' Discuss the benefits and drawbacks of the Docklands Development Scheme or any other urban redevelopment programme you have studied. (6)

(d) 'Large cities have many different problems.' Outline the problems which exist in London or any other city in an economically developed country you have studied. (5)

(25)

Figure 6.8A Traffic congestion in a city

8 **(a)** Figure 6.8A shows traffic congestion in a city in an economically developed country. Outline the economic and environmental problems associated with traffic congestion. (5)

(b) Traffic congestion is usually greatest in the oldest parts of cities. Explain why. (4)

(c) Discuss the effectiveness of the different measures which city planners can take to discourage people from taking their cars into the centres of cities. (6)

(d) Look at the OS map of York on the inside back cover.

i. Name and describe two roads which have been built to try and reduce traffic congestion in the centre of York. (3)

ii. Outline the conflicts which might have arisen over the construction of these roads. (3)

iii. Figure 6.8B shows the River Foss in York. Referring to activities included in Figure 6.8B outline the impact of the River Foss on traffic flows within York. (4)

(25)

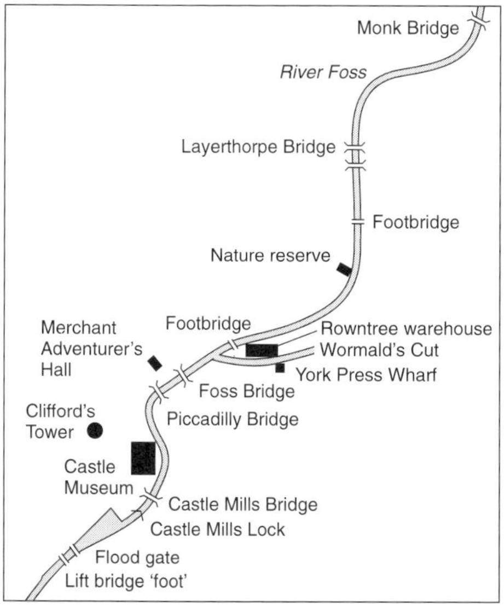

Figure 6.8B The River Foss in York

'millionaire city'	*population (million)*
Mexico City	25.2
São Paulo	24.0
Tokyo	20.2
Calcutta	16.5
Bombay	16.0
New York	15.8
Shanghai	14.3
Seoul	13.8
Tehran	13.6
Rio de Janeiro	13.3

Figure 6.9A The world's largest 'millionaire cities'

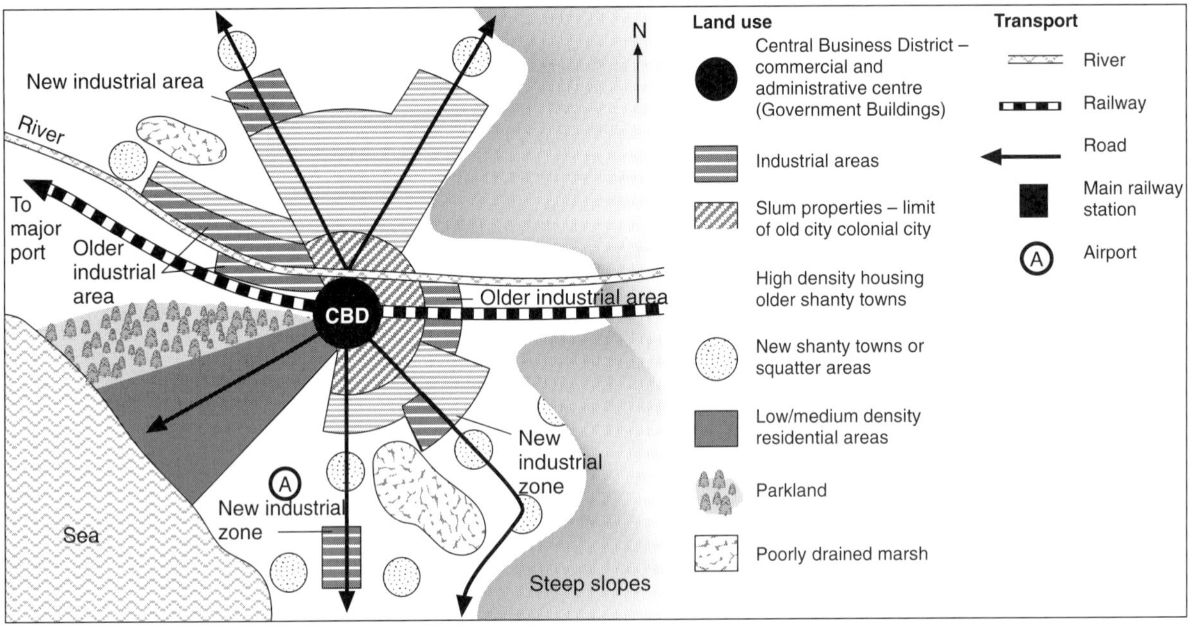

Figure 6.9B The layout of a city in an economically developing country

9 (a) Figure 6.9A shows the layout of a city in an economically developing country.

i. Explain the location of the squatter settlements. (3)

ii. State the reasons for the development of squatter settlements in cities in economically developing countries. (4)

iii. 'The awful conditions which exist in the squatter settlements pose the greatest problems for many cities in economically developing countries.'
Describe and explain the conditions in a typical squatter settlement. (6)

(b) Examine Figure 6.9B which shows the world's largest 'millionaire cities'.

i. State the meaning of the term 'millionaire city'. (2)

ii. 'Most of the world's largest cities are in economically developing countries.' Explain why so many of the world's largest millionaire cities are in economically developing countries. (2)

(c) Examine Figure 6.9C which describes a self-help scheme to improve conditions in Karachi, Pakistan.
Discuss the advantages of self-help schemes for improving conditions in shanty towns.
(6)

(25)

Residents in a poor housing area on the outskirts of Karachi have grouped together to build a new sewage system. Each householder paid around £30 for the new sewage disposal system which will help to ensure they have access to clean water for drinking, cleaning and washing. Costs for the new system were kept down because of the willingness of local people to do most of the construction work themselves. A report from the World Bank estimates that two million children die each year, in countries throughout the world, from illnesses caused by dirty drinking and washing water.

Figure 6.9C A self-help scheme in Karachi

7 Industry and Trade

Key words

assembly plant a factory in which goods are assembled from different components which are made in other factories; a good example of an assembly plant is a car plant
assisted area an area which receives Government help to attract new industries
balance of trade the difference between the value of a country's imports and the value of its exports
capital the money required for setting up and developing a business
de-industrialisation the declining importance of manufacturing industry in more economically developed countries
derelict land land which was once used but which has now been abandoned, for example: a disused industrial site
enterprise zone an area which offers special incentives to attract new industries
exports goods which are sold to other countries
greenfield site a site, for a new factory for example, which lies in the countryside
high-tech industry an industry, such as computer making, which uses advanced equipment
imports goods which are bought from other countries
industrial estate an area of modern factories
infrastructure the framework of roads, railways, power and water supplies
multinational companies large companies which have factories and offices in many different countries; examples of multinational companies include IBM and Toyota
new industrial landscape an estate of modern factories with clean air and much greenery
oil refinery a large plant where crude oil is refined into petrol and other oil-based products
old industrial landscape areas of factories and houses with little greenery and much air pollution
primary industries activities such as farming, fishing and mining which involve taking resources from the land or sea
primary products raw materials such as timber and mineral-ores which are used to make manufactured goods
raw materials materials such as steel and wood which are used to make finished goods
science parks modern industrial areas, often situated near to universities, with research laboratories and high-tech industries
secondary industries activities such as steelmaking and shipbuilding which involve making or manufacturing goods from raw materials
secondary products manufactured goods such as cars and computers
sunrise industry an industry which is growing in importance
sunset industry an industry which is declining in importance
tariff a tax which is put on goods entering a country
tertiary industries activities, such as serving in shops or driving buses, which involve providing services
trade deficit when the value of imports exceeds the value of exports
trade gap the difference between what a country exports and what it imports
trade interdependence when countries depend on each other for buying and selling
trade surplus when the value of exports exceeds the value of imports
trading buying and selling

CORE QUESTIONS

1 (a) Study Figure 7.1A which shows a painting of an old industrial landscape in the north of England.

i. Outline three ways in which the industries shown in the painting are harming the environment. (3)

ii. Many of the industries in the painting are heavy industries. State the meaning of the term 'heavy industries'. Give two examples of heavy industries. (3)

iii. State three ways in which a new industrial landscape is different from an old industrial landscape. (3)

(b) Figure 7.1B is a flow diagram showing the inputs, processes and outputs for a steelworks. Apart from workers state two other inputs which are required for producing steel. (2)

(c) During the past 250 years the 'best location' for a steelworks has changed from woodland areas to coalfields to coastal sites. Give reasons for these changes. (3)

(d) Figure 7.1C shows a derelict steelworks. Outline the possible effects of a closing steelworks on:

i. the steelworkers; (2)

ii. shops and services in the settlement in which the steelworks is located. (2)

iii. the environment. (2)

(20)

Figure 7.1A An old industrial landscape

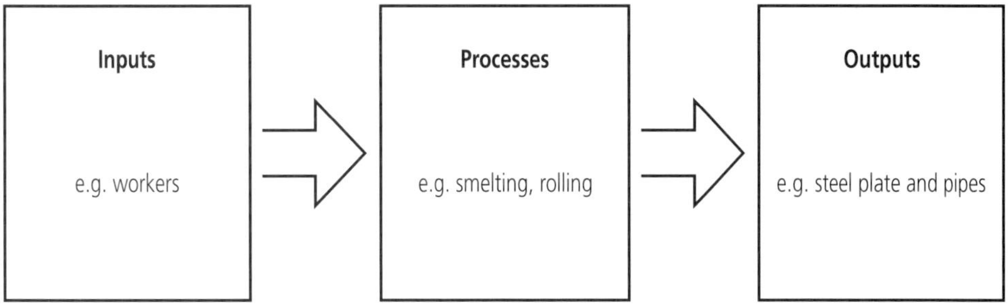

Figure 7.1B The inputs and outputs for a steelworks

Figure 7.1C A derelict steelworks

2 For this question you should look at the OS map of the York area on the inside back cover.

(a) Examine the works in grid square 5851. Is this an old works or a new works? Give two reasons for your answer. (4)

(b) Infrastructure is the roads, railways, ports, electricity supply lines, water supply and other facilities which factories require. What infrastructure is available for industry in grid square 5753? (3)

(c) Grid squares 6150 and 5856 provide two possible sites for a new industrial estate for high-tech industries. Which of these grid squares provides the best site? Give three reasons for your choice. (4)

(d) Figure 7.2A shows a disused woollen mill in the countryside around York.

i. Suggest two reasons why the mill was built next to a river. (2)

ii. Outline two possible reasons why the mill was forced to close. (4)

(e) Industries can be categorised as primary, secondary or tertiary. Give the name, and a four-figure grid reference, of an example of:

i. a primary industry; (1)

ii. a secondary industry; (1)

iii. a tertiary industry. (1)

(20)

Figure 7.2A A disused woollen mill

3 **(a)** Figure 7.3A shows some of the factors which affect the location of a factory. State:

i. one physical factor; (1)
ii. one economic factor; (1)
iii. one political factor. (1)

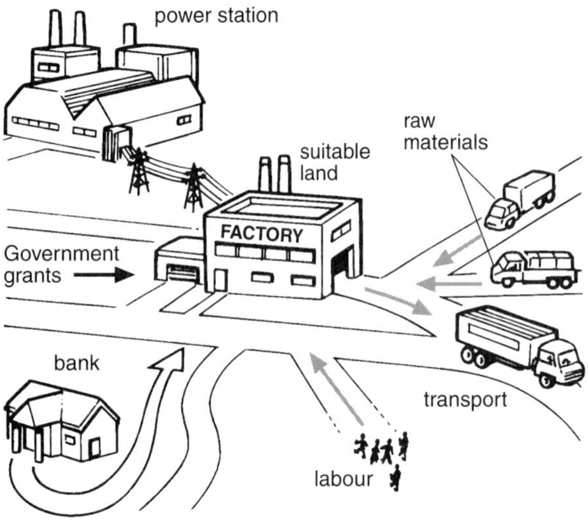

Figure 7.3A Some of the factors which affect the location of a factory

(b) Look at Figure 7.3B which shows three possible sites for an oil refinery. Which site (X, Y or Z) is the best site for an oil refinery?

i. Give three reasons for your choice. (4)
ii. What benefits would an oil refinery bring to an area? (2)
iii. What disadvantages might an oil refinery create for an area? (2)

(c) Examine Figure 7.3C which shows the location of Japanese-owned car assembly plants, and their component factories, in the United Kingdom.

i. Outline what is meant by the term 'assembly plant'. (2)
ii. Describe the distribution of the United Kingdom's car assembly plants and component factories. (3)
iii. Give two reasons for the distribution of the United Kingdom's car assembly plants and component factories. (4)

(20)

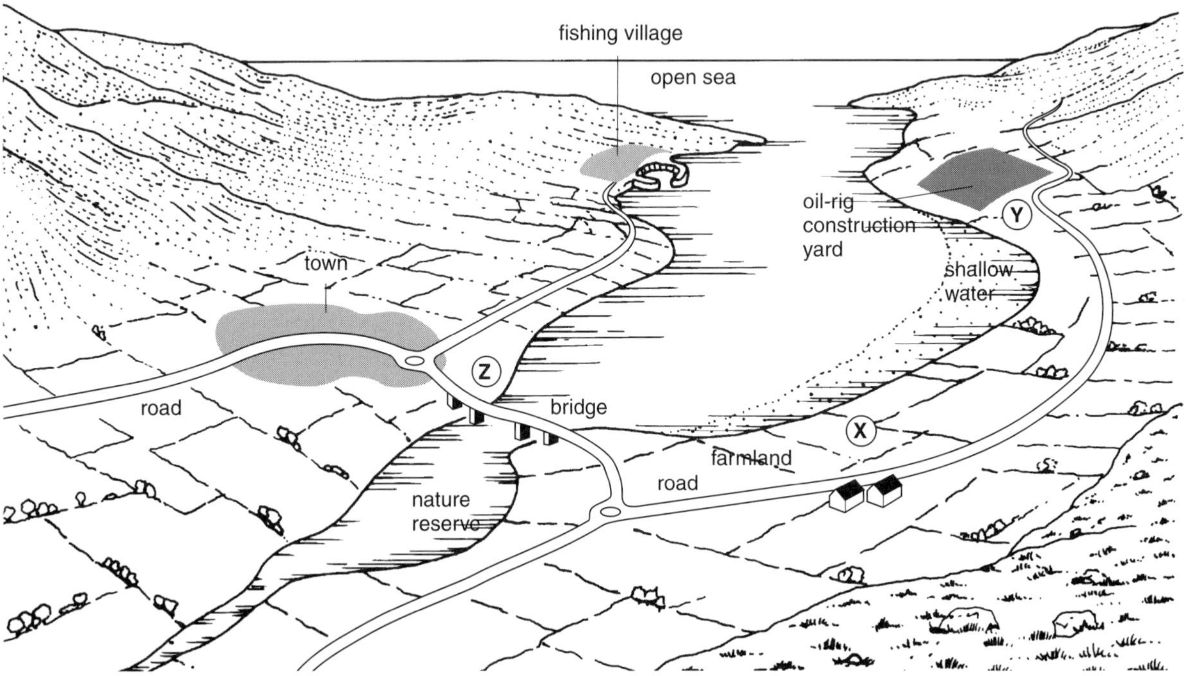

Figure 7.3B Three possible sites for an oil refinery

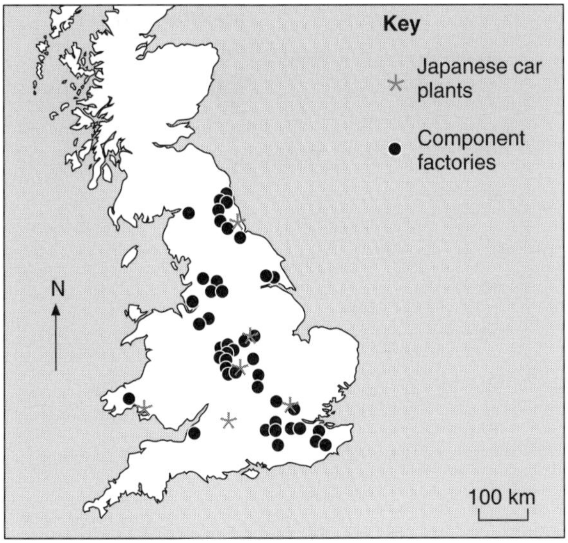

Figure 7.3C The location of Japanese-owned car assembly plants and component factories

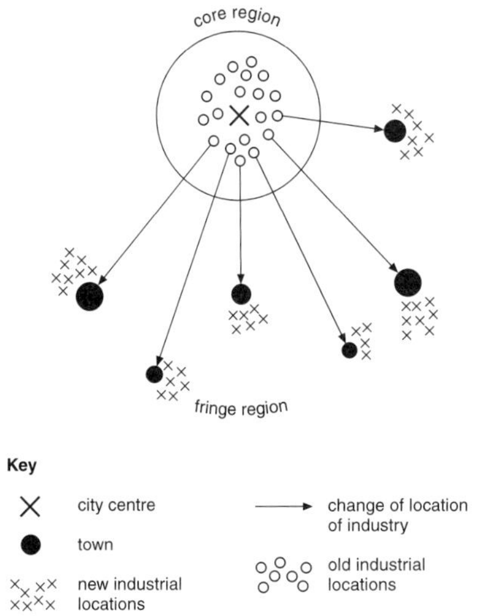

Figure 7.4B A model of change to the location of industry

EXTENSION QUESTIONS

4 (a) Figure 7.4A shows changes to the coal industry in the United Kingdom.

i. Describe and explain the changes which have taken place. (6)

ii. Outline the economic and social impact of the declining coal industry on coalmining communities. (4)

(b) Study Figure 7.4B which shows a model of change to the location of industry. Describe and explain the changes shown by the model. (5)

(c) Use named examples to help you describe two ways in which the Government can help areas affected by declining industry. (4)

(d) Figure 7.4C shows new high-tech industries in 'Silicon Glen' in Central Scotland.

i. What are the locational requirements for high-tech industries? (3)

ii. What benefits can high-tech industries bring to an area? (3)

(25)

Figure 7.4C New high-tech industries in 'Silicon Glen'

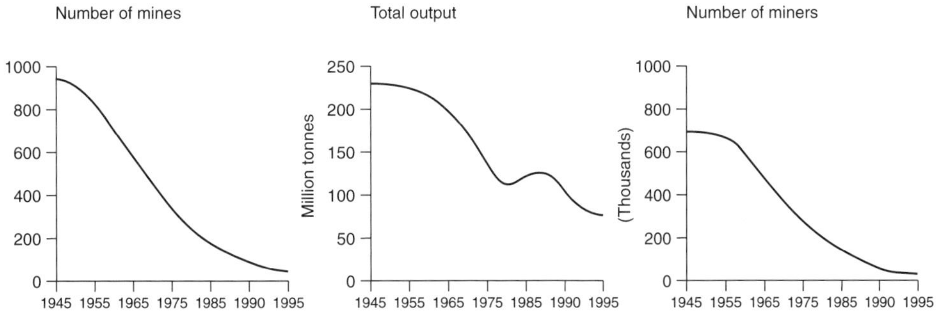

Figure 7.4A Changes to the coal industry in the United Kingdom

5 (a) Study Figure 7.5A and Figure 7.5B

i. Why do so many industries have river-side locations? (3)

ii. Discuss the effects that some industries have on rivers such as the Tagus. (3)

iii. What would reduce industrial pollution in the Tagus Estuary? (3)

(b) Using Figure 7.5C, compare and contrast the industrial structures of Kenya and USA. (4)

(c) Explain why industrial development remains slow in many economically developing countries. (4)

(d) Figure 7.5D shows world exports.

i. Use named examples to help you outline the difference between primary products and secondary products. (3)

ii. Describe and explain the pattern of world exports. (5)

(25)

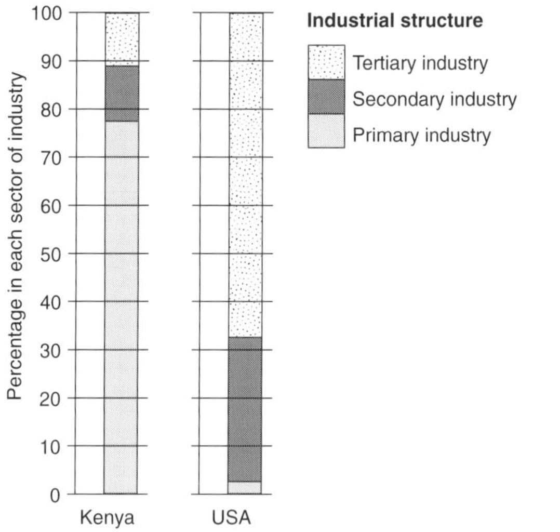

Figure 7.5C The industrial structure of Kenya and the United States

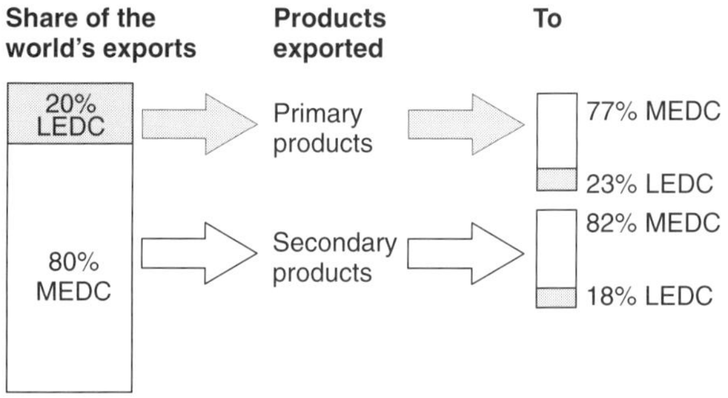

LEDC – Less economically developed countries

MEDC – More economically developed countries

Figure 7.5D World exports

Figure 7.5B Part of an industrial complex on the Tagus Estuary

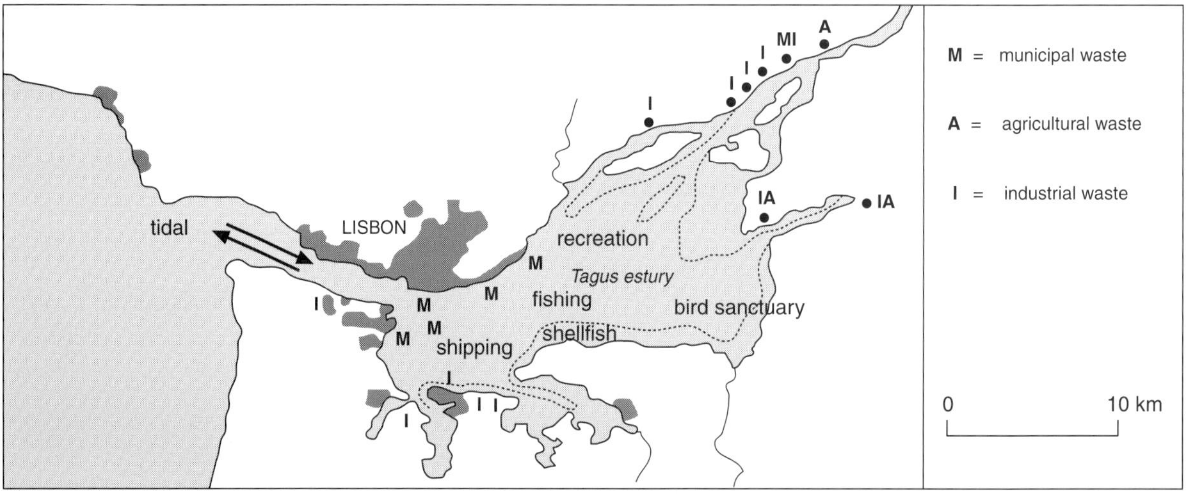

Figure 7.5A Pollution in the Tagus Estuary

6 (a) Figure 7.6A provides information about the Pacific Coast industrial region in Japan while Figure 7.6B shows how Japanese industry in this region changed between 1965 and 1995.

i. Discuss the factors which have helped industry to develop in Japan's Pacific Coast region. (4)

ii. Explain the changes which have taken place in this industrial region. (4)

(b) The Toyota Motor Corporation, one of Japan's leading companies, is a multi-national company with factories in many different parts of the world.

i. Explain why large companies such as the Toyota Motor Corporation have factories in many different parts of the world. (4)

ii. What benefits do multi-national companies bring to a country? (3)

iii. What are the drawbacks associated with the presence of multi-national companies in a country? (3)

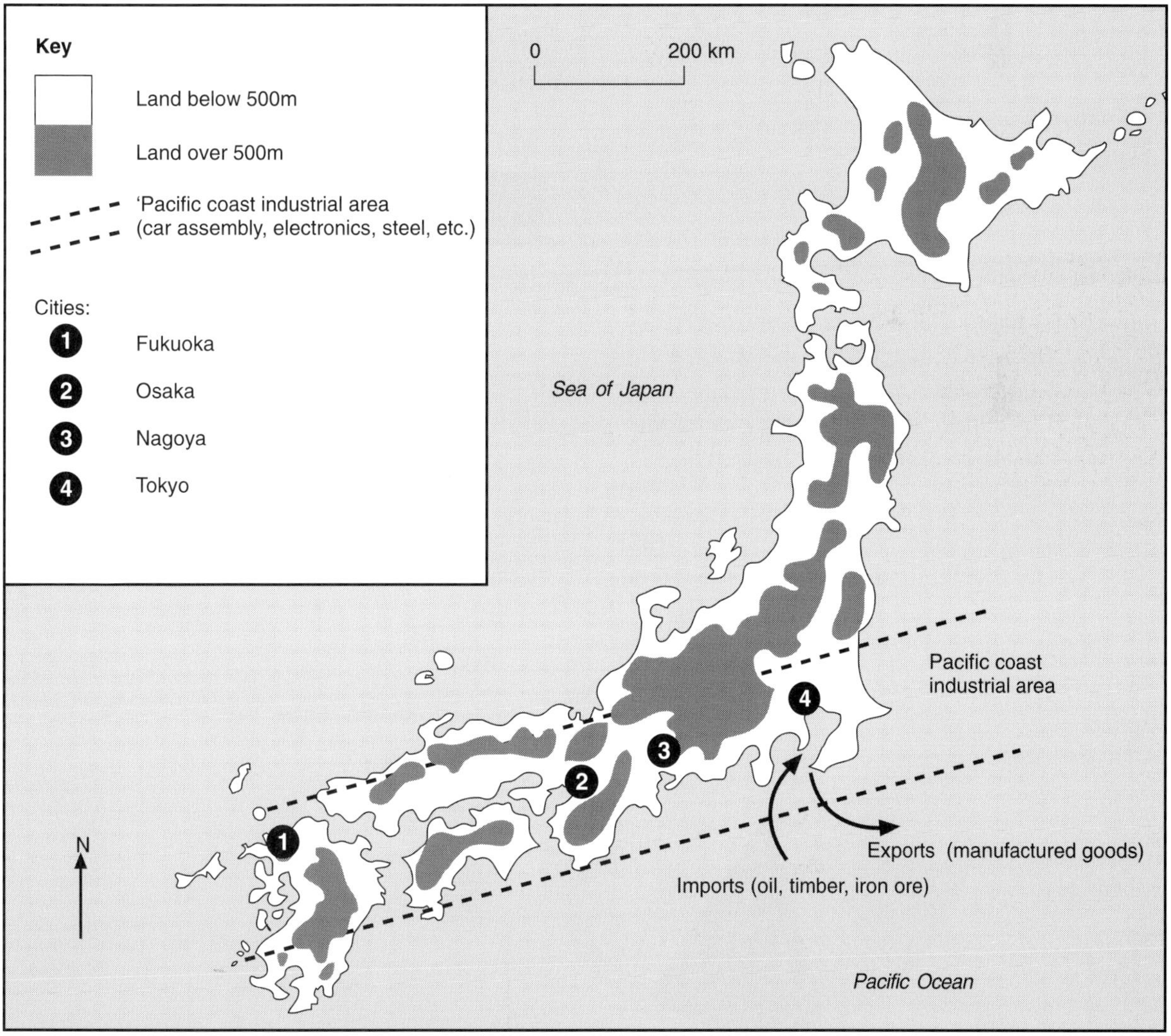

Figure 7.6A Information about the Pacific Coast industrial region in Japan

Types of industry	Examples	% of workforce		Key for graphs
		1965	1995	
Unskilled – using many workers	Clothing, shoes, toys, shops	52	11	
Industries using many raw materials	Steel, plastics, chemicals	13	22	
Industries using much machinery and labour	TV sets, cars, radios	25	25	
Industries based on knowledge	Computers, instruments	10	42	

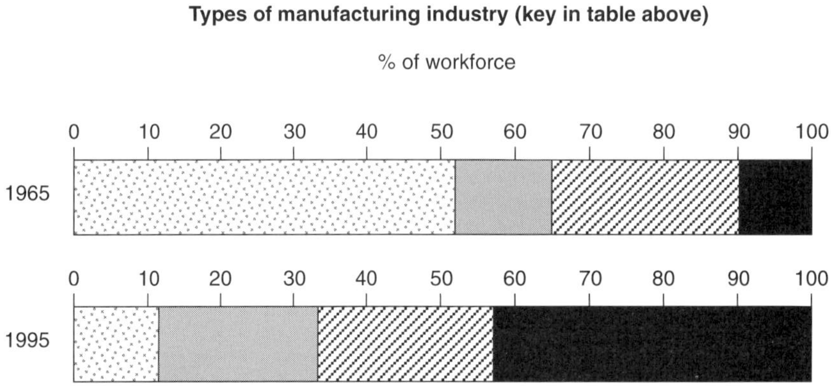

Figure 7.6B Changes to industry in Japan's Pacific Coast region

(c) Study Figure 7.6C which shows world trade.
 i. Describe and explain Japan's share of world trade. (4)
 ii. Use named examples to help you outline the meaning of the term 'trade inter-dependence'. (3)

(25)

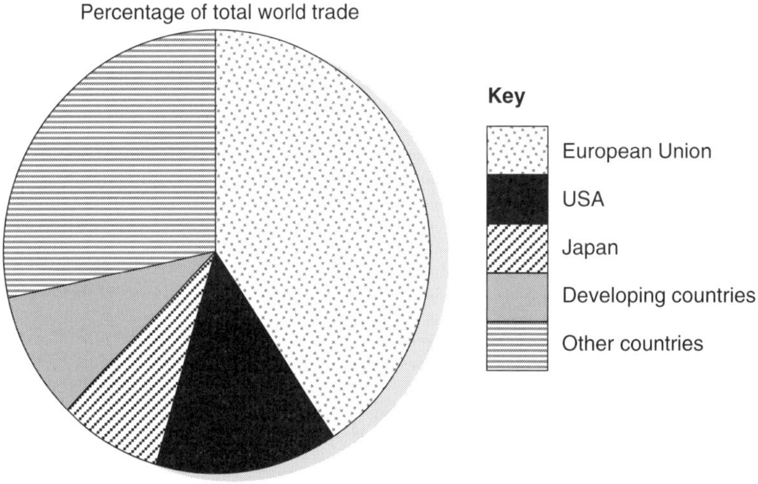

Figure 7.6C World trade

8 Farming

Key words

agribusiness the organisation of a farm as a business
agriculture the use of the land for growing plants and rearing animals
arable land land which is used for growing crops
aspect the direction in which a slope faces
cash crops crops which are grown for sale
commercial farming farming for money
consolidation the joining of smaller fields and smaller farms to make larger more profitable fields and farms
crop rotation moving crops from field to field every few years or so in order to maintain the fertility of the soil
dairy farming the rearing of animals in order to produce milk and milk-based products such as butter and cheese
extensive agriculture a type of farming, such as sheep farming, which covers a large area but has low yields
fertiliser a substance which makes the soil more fertile
fodder crops crops which are grown for animals to eat
Green Revolution the farming improvements, including new seeds, fertilisers and equipment, which have enabled farmers in less economically developed countries to produce more food
horticulture the growing of flowers, fruit and vegetables
industrial crops crops, such as cotton, which are grown for use in industry
inputs the land, seeds, fertilisers, machines, workers and other requirements for farming
intensive farming a type of farming, such as market gardening, which has a high level of inputs of capital and labour to produce high yields
irrigation additional water, from wells, reservoirs and sprinkler systems, to overcome droughts or low rainfall
market garden a small farm which produces soft fruits, flowers and vegetables
market town a town, surrounded by good farmland, which provides services for farmers
miracle seeds seeds for rice and other crops which provide higher crop-yields
mixed farming farming which involves different types of agricultural activities including growing crops and rearing animals
monoculture the cultivation of one crop
organic farming farming which doesn't use artificial fertilisers or pesticides
outputs the crops and other products which are produced by farms
pastoral land land which is left as grass for animals to eat
plantation a large farm, usually in the tropics, which grows crops such as rubber and coffee
relief the shape and height of the land
set-aside land land which has been taken out of cultivation in order to reduce the over-production of crops
subsistence farming farming which only produces enough food to feed farmers and their families
transhumance the seasonal movement of animals from fields on valley floors to the upland pastures; this enables the lower fields to be used for growing winter fodder

CORE QUESTIONS

1 (a) Study Figure 8.1A which shows variations in relief, climate and farming in mainland Britain.

State the main type of farming in the:

i. wettest parts of mainland Britain; (1)

ii. driest parts of mainland Britain; (1)

iii. highest parts of mainland Britain; (1)

iv. lowest and warmest parts of mainland Britain. (1)

(b) Look at Figure 8.1B which shows a dairy farm system. State:

i. two physical inputs; (2)

ii. two human inputs; (2)

iii. two processes (other than milking). (2)

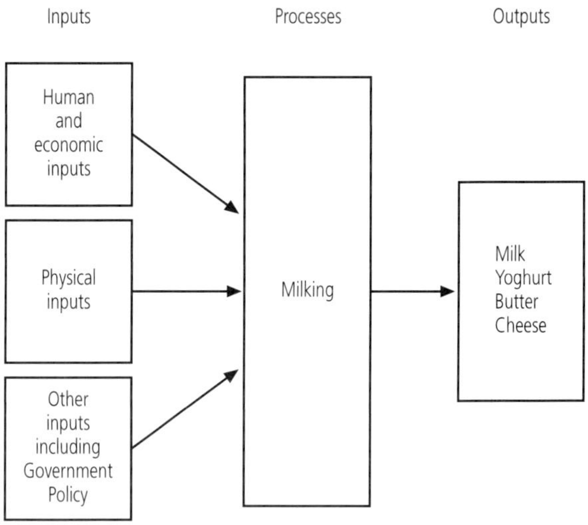

Figure 8.1B A dairy farm system

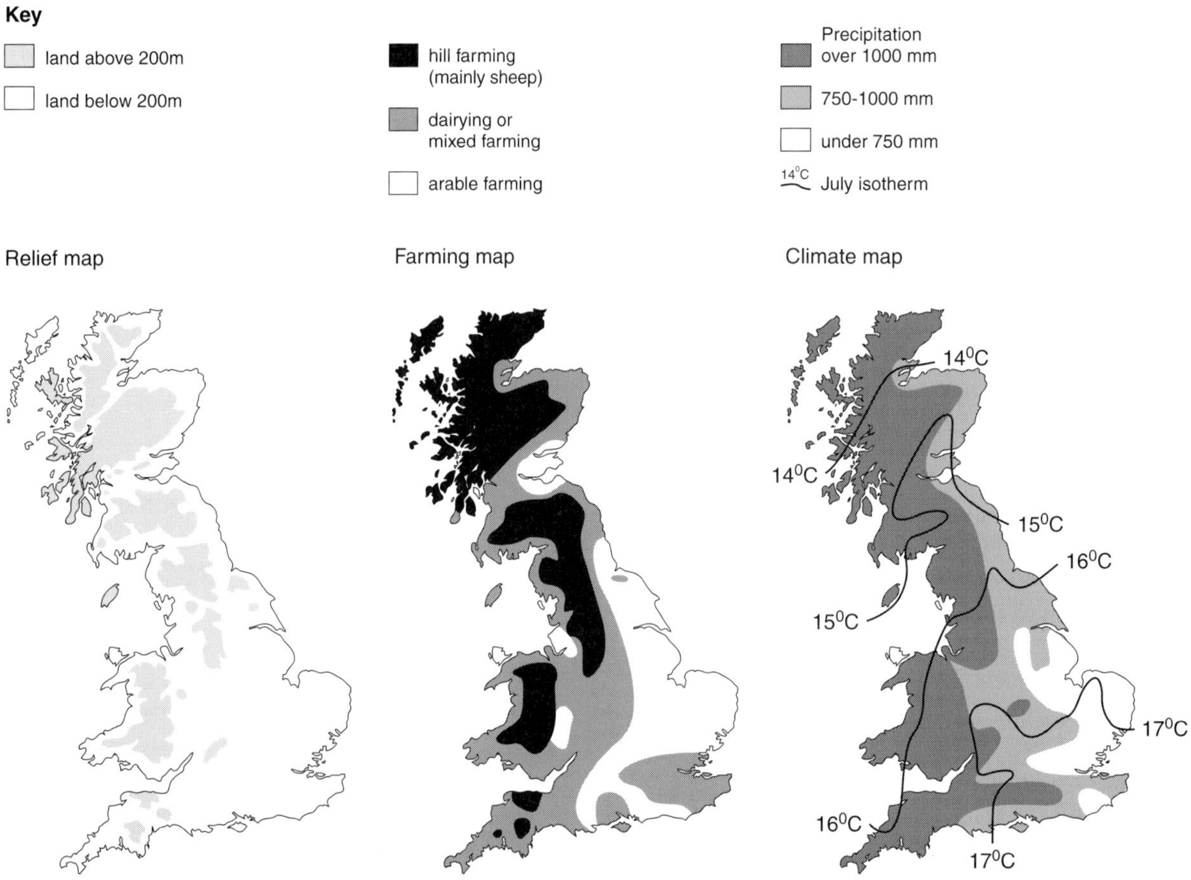

Figure 8.1A Variations in relief, climate and farming in mainland Britain

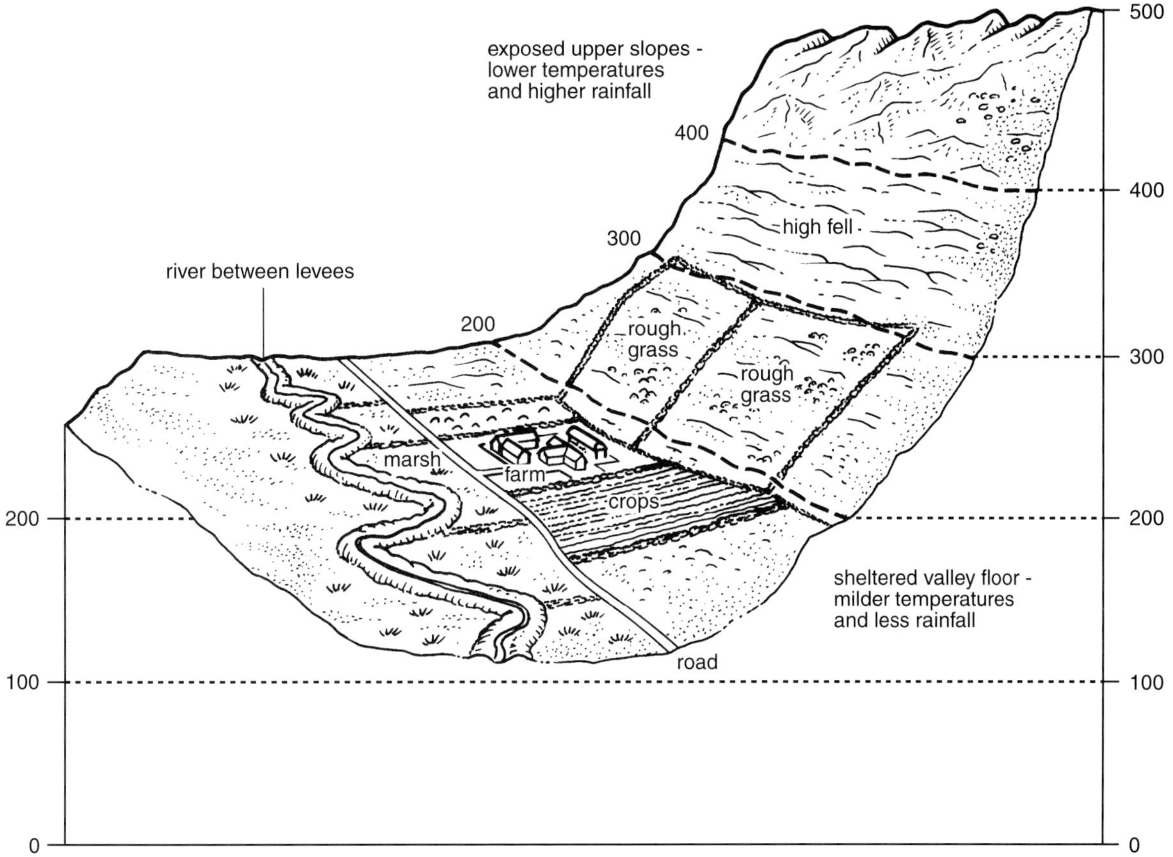

Figure 8.1C A farm in the Lake District

(c) Figure 8.1C shows a farm in the Lake District of north west England.

i. Which part of the farm is used for growing crops? (1)

ii. Why is this part of the farm the most suitable area for growing crops? Give two reasons. (2)

iii. Why are no crops being grown next to the river? (1)

iv. What might the area of rough grass be used for? (1)

v. What problems are caused by the climate in this area? (2)

vi. This farm lies in a popular tourist area. State two benefits this might bring to the farm. (2)

vii. State one disadvantage of farming in a popular tourist area. (1)

(20)

2 (a) Figure 8.2A shows some of the ways in which farmers overcome problems with the land and the climate.
State one way farmers can overcome the problem of:

i. long dry spells; (1)

ii. a river which frequently floods; (1)

iii. infertile soil; (1)

iv. insects destroying crops; (1)

v. land which is marshy; (1)

vi. a lack of flat land; (1)

vii. a lack of knowledge about modern farming methods. (1)

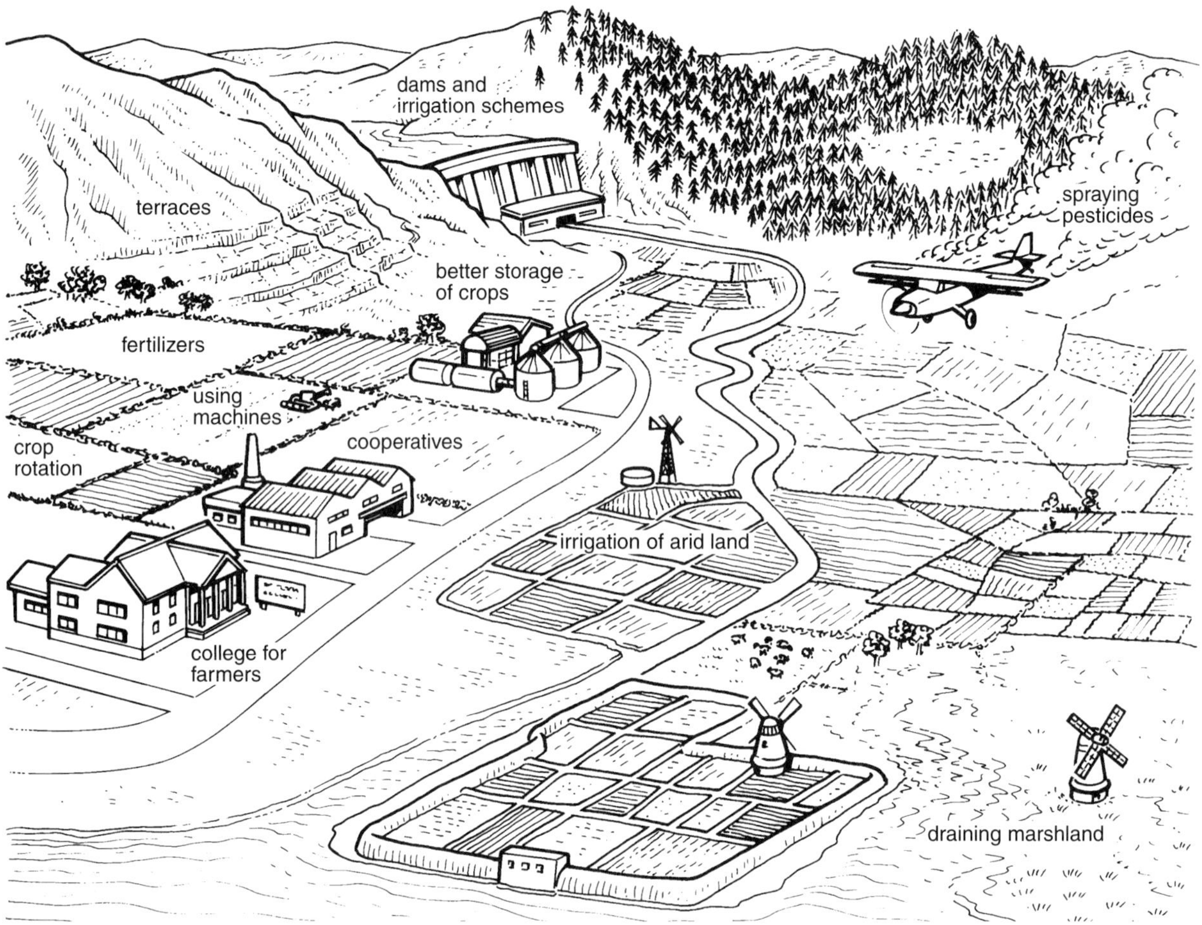

Figure 8.2A Ways in which farmers overcome problems with the land and climate

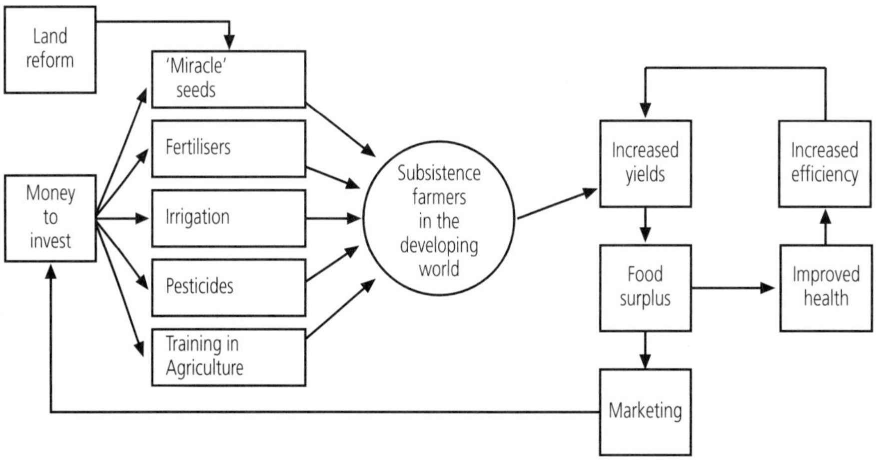

Figure 8.2B The effects of the 'Green Revolution'

(b) Figure 8.2B shows the effects of the 'Green Revolution'.
   i. What is the 'Green Revolution'? (2)
   ii. Describe how the 'Green Revolution' has benefited farmers in economically developing countries. (3)
   iii. Outline one problem which has arisen in some areas because of the 'Green Revolution'. (1)

(c) Figure 8.2C shows factors influencing farming. State:
   i. two physical factors; (2)
   ii. two human factors; (2)
   iii. one political factor. (1)

(d) State two ways in which Governments can help farmers. (2)

(20)

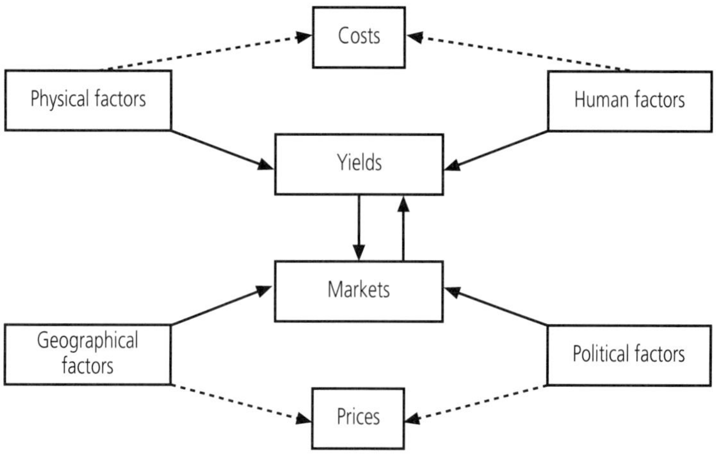

Figure 8.2C Factors influencing farming

EXTENSION QUESTIONS

3 (a) Examine Figure 8.3A which shows a rural landscape.
Draw an annotated sketch to help you describe and explain the advantages and disadvantages of this landscape for farming. (6)

(b) Study Figure 8.3B which shows some of the changes which have taken place in the British countryside during the past fifty years.
   i. Account for these changes. (6)
   ii. For any *two* of these changes explain why some people have opposed the changes. (4)
   iii. Describe ways in which agricultural change has led to rural depopulation in some parts of the British Isles. (4)

(c) Many farms are organised as agribusinesses. Outline, with the help of examples, the meaning of the term 'agribusiness'. (5)

(25)

Figure 8.3A A rural landscape

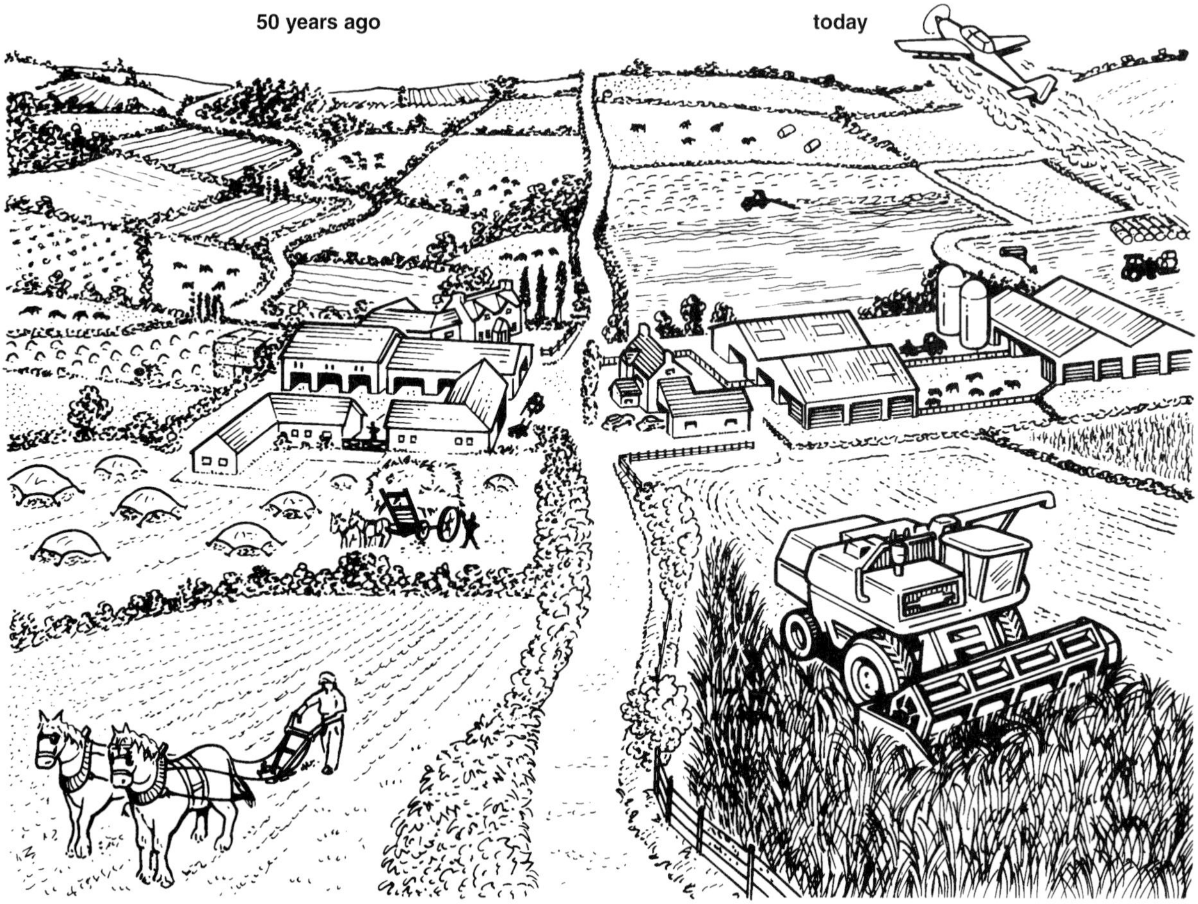

Figure 8.3B Changes to the British countryside

4 For this question you should look at the OS map of the York area on the inside back cover.

(a) Describe the site and situation of Brecks Farm (598567). (4)

(b) Grange Farm (639496), along with other farms in the south-east corner of the map, has been affected by the construction of the A64(T) road. Outline ways in which farming will have been affected by the road. (4)

(c) Eastfield Farm (566488) is situated beside a public footpath. State the advantages and disadvantages of this footpath for the farmer. (4)

(d) Identify, and suggest reasons for, the type of farming carried out at 564546. (3)

(e) Some of the arable land in the York area is 'set-aside land'. State what is meant by 'set-aside land' and suggest ways in which farmers in the York area could use this land. (4)

(f) Figure 8.4 shows a plan of a farm next to York.
Outline ways in which a site next to a city will affect this farm. (6)

(25)

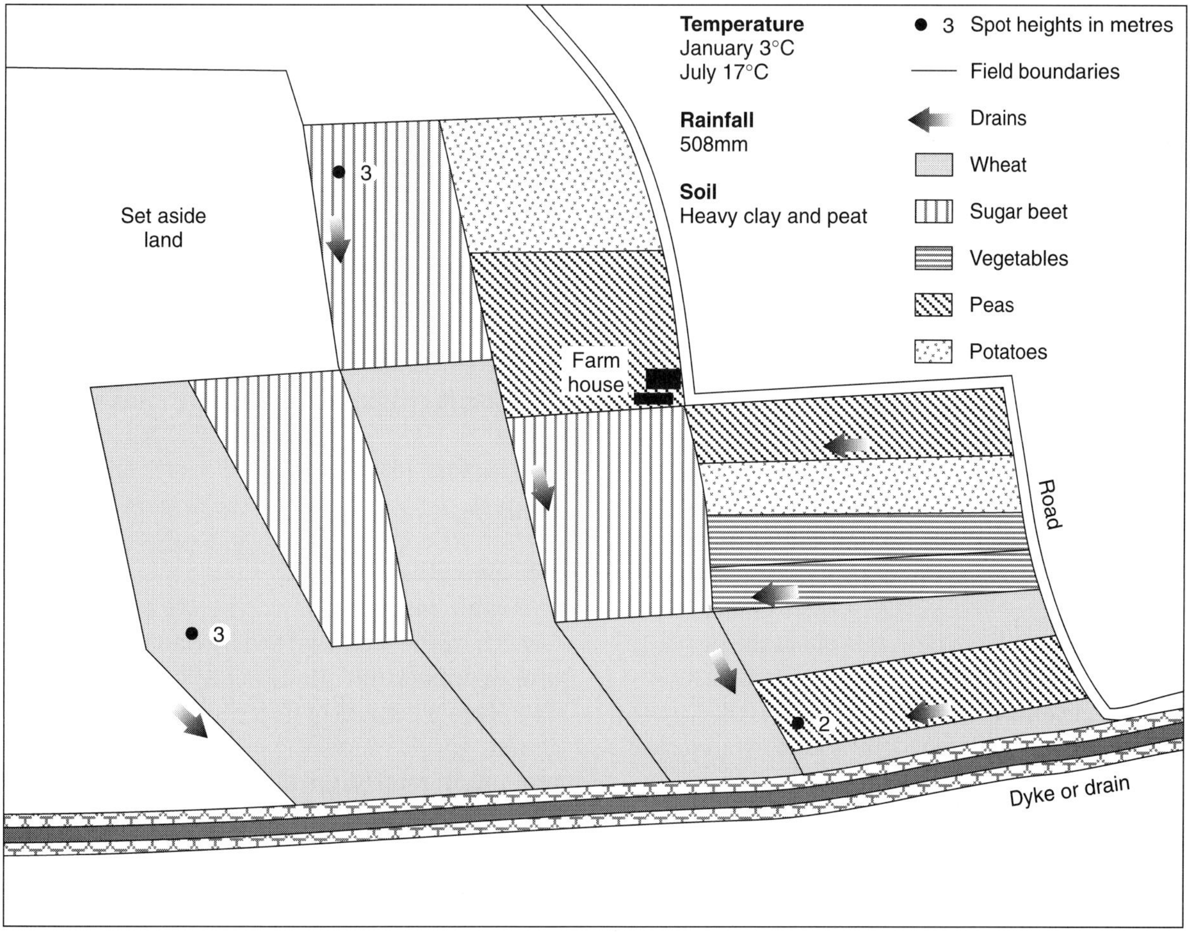

Figure 8.4 A plan of a farm next to York

9 Population

Key words

active population the population of working age, for example: age 16 to 65 (these ages vary from country to country)
age structure the composition of a population according to age
ageing population a population in which the average age is rising and which contains a large percentage of people over the age of 60
birth rate the number of births per 1000 people
census a count of the number of people living in a country
death rate the number of deaths per 1000 people
demographic transition model a model which shows changing rates of fertility, mortality and natural increase
emigration the movement of people out of a country
fertility ratio the ratio of children to women
immigration the movement of people into a country
life expectancy the average number of years a new born baby can expect to live
literacy rate the percentage of the population who have been taught how to read and write
migration the movement of people from one place to another
natural increase the birth rate minus the death rate – in other words the increase in population
natural resources the parts of the physical environment, including forests or minerals such as coal and oil, which are useful to people
negative areas empty areas where the land is difficult for settlement
non-renewable resources resources such as coal and oil which can't be replaced once they have been used up
overpopulation too many people for a particular area to support; this may arise if the population has outstripped the available resources or if the resources have become exhausted
population the number of people in a city, country or region
population change the increase or decrease in population
population density the number of people per square kilometre of land
population distribution the way in which population is spread throughout a country or region
population explosion a large and rapid increase in population
population pyramid a bar graph which shows the age and sex composition of a population
positive areas crowded areas where the land and climate is suitable for settlement
pull factors reasons why people are attracted to an area
push factors reasons why people leave an area
refugees people who are forced to leave their home areas because of a war, a natural disaster or some other danger
renewable resources resources such as water which can be used over and over again
rural depopulation the decrease in population of rural areas because of migration or falling birth rates
rural-urban migration the movement of people from small rural settlements to towns and cities
urban-rural migration the movement of people from towns and cities to smaller rural settlements
youthful population a population in which the average age is low

CORE QUESTIONS

1 (a) Figure 9.1A shows population change for six countries.

i. State the 'natural increase' for India. (1)

ii. Give two reasons why some countries have high birth rates. (2)

iii. Give two reasons why some countries have low death rates. (2)

Table 9.1A Population change

Country	Birth Rate per 1000	Death Rate per 1000	Natural population increase per 1000
Tanzania	48	15	33
Bangladesh	37	13	24
India	30	10	–
Argentina	21	8	13
China	18	7	–
Italy	10	10	0

(b) Examine Figure 9.1B which shows a population pyramid for France.

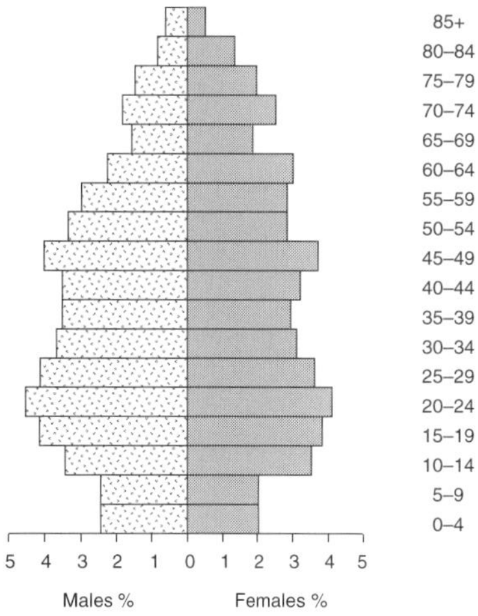

Figure 9.1B A population pyramid for France

i. Which age group has the highest percentage of males? (1)

ii. State one age group which can be categorised as 'dependents'. (1)

iii. State one age group which can be categorised as 'active'. (1)

iv. Give two pieces of evidence which indicate that France is an economically developed country. (2)

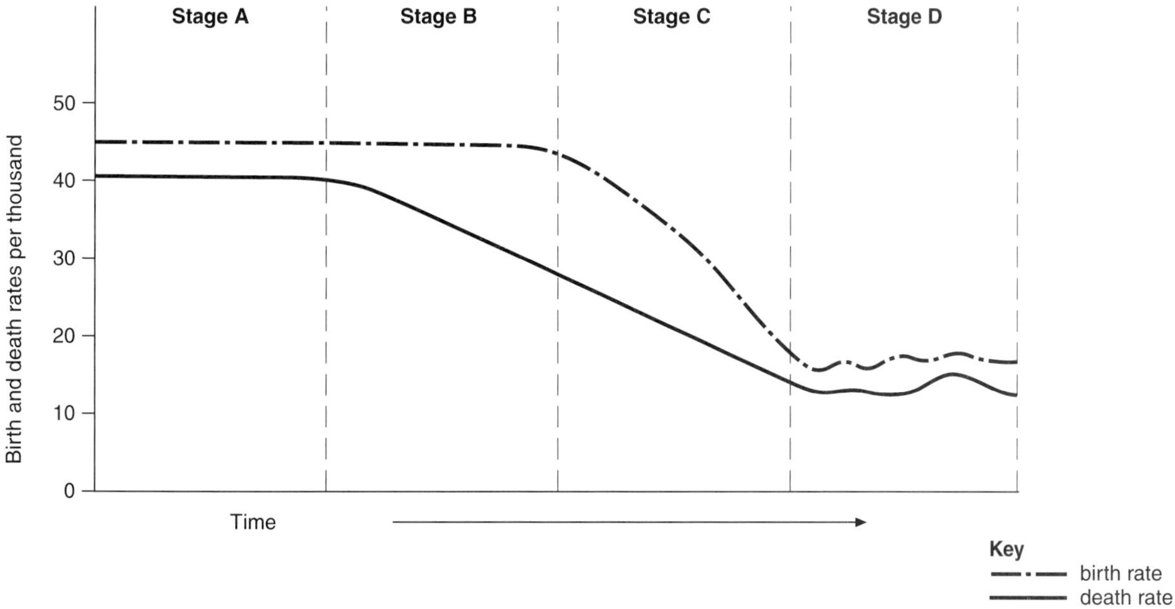

Figure 9.1C The demographic transition model

(c) Figure 9.1C shows the demographic transition model.
Use the model to help you copy and complete the following table:

	birth rate	death rate	natural increase
stage A	high	________	
stage B	________	falling	________
stage C	________	falling	________
stage D	________	________	low

choose from: high low falling increasing. (4)

(d) The world has experienced a 'population explosion'?
i. What is a 'population explosion'? (2)
ii. What are the main causes of the world's 'population explosion'? (4)

(20)

(b) Study Figure 9.2A which shows two population pyramids.
i. Which of the population pyramids (X or Y) is for an economically developing country?
Give two reasons for your choice. (3)
ii. Which of the population pyramids (X or Y) is for an economically developed country?
Give two reasons for your choice. (3)

(c) Examine Figure 9.2B which shows natural population increase.
i. Which continent has the most countries with the highest rate of population increase? (1)

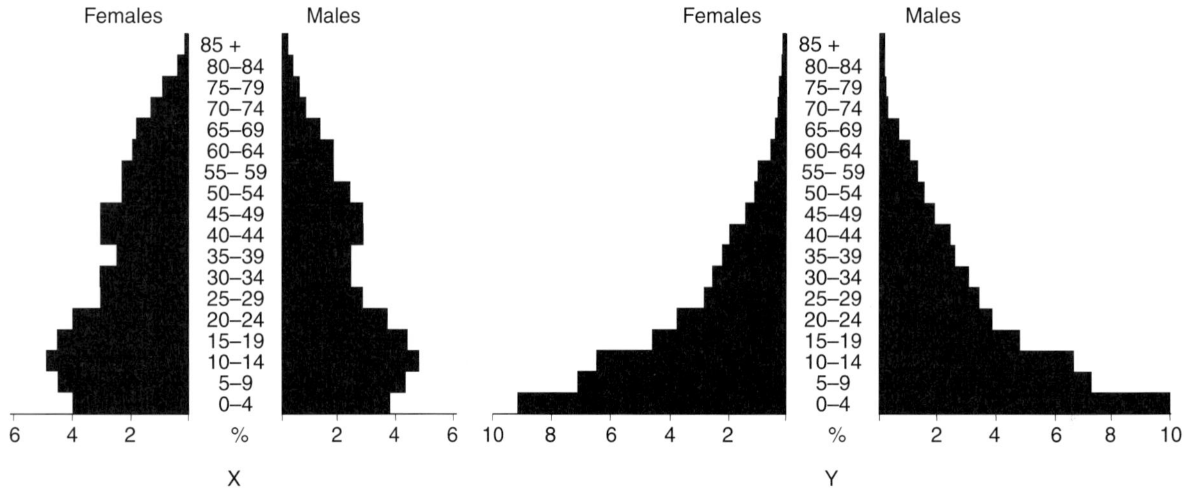

Figure 9.2A Two population pyramids

2 (a) Some parts of the world have high population densities while other parts have low population densities. Name and describe a part of the world that has:
i. a high population density
ii. a low population density (6)

ii. Explain why some continents have high rates of population increase. (3)
iii. Name two continents which have low rates of population increase. (2)
iv. For one of the continents you named in your answer to (c)iii. give reasons why the rate of population increase is low. (2)

(20)

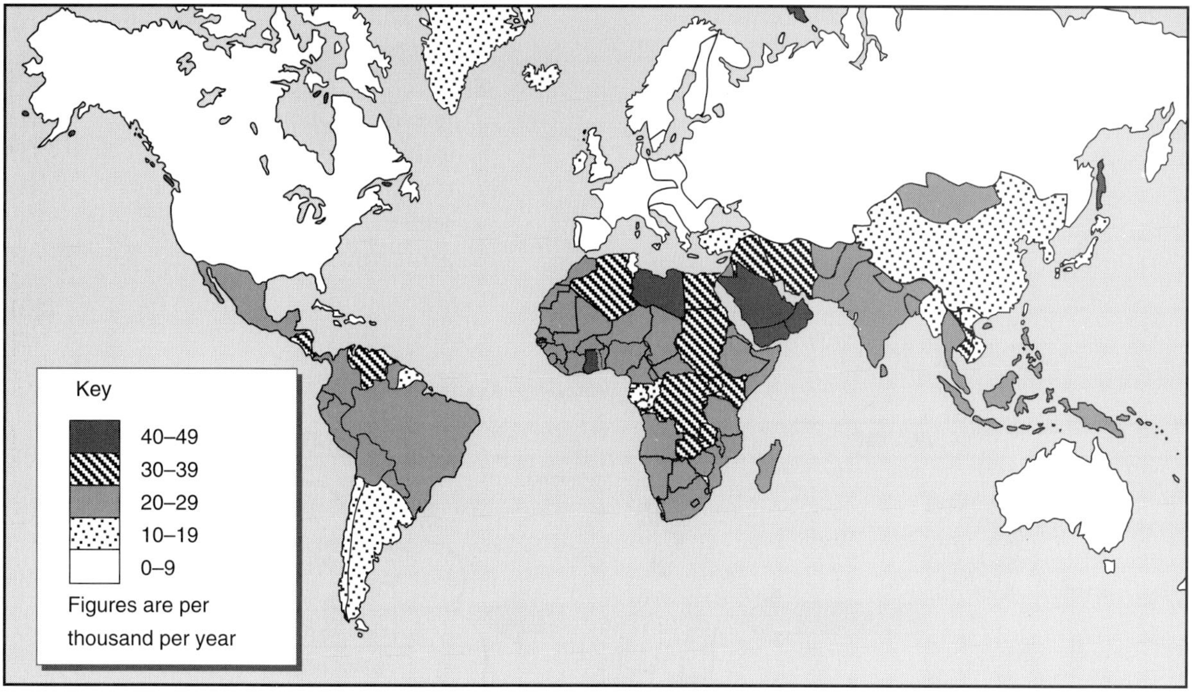

Figure 9.2B Natural population increase

3 **(a)** Examine Figure 9.3A which shows world population.
Use the graph to help you copy and complete the following table:

year	population of MEDC (millions)	population of LEDC (millions)	world population (millions)	
1850	______	800	______	
1950	1000	______	______	
2050	______	______	10 000	(3)

MEDC – more economically developed countries
LEDC – less economically developed countries

(b) Look at Figure 9.3B which shows some of the reasons why people migrate in economically developing countries.

i. Give two 'push' factors. (2)
ii. Give two 'pull' factors. (2)

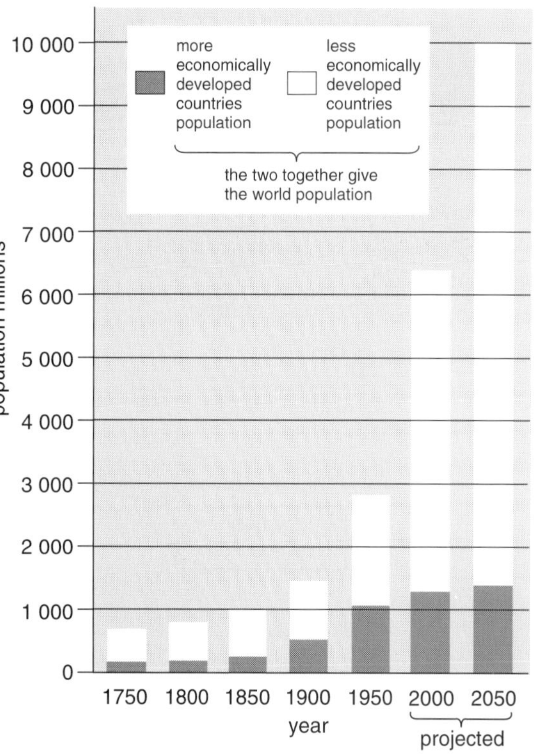

Figure 9.3A World population

iii. State two 'obstacles' which discourage people from leaving their home areas. (2)
iv. Outline the problems 'greater urbanisation' creates for the city. (3)
v. Outline the problems 'rural depopulation' creates for the village. (3)

(c) Study Figure 9.3C which shows different types of migration. Give one named example of:
i. forced migration; (1)
ii. daily movements; (1)
iii. seasonal migration; (1)
iv. semi-permanent migration; (1)
v. permanent migration. (1)

(20)

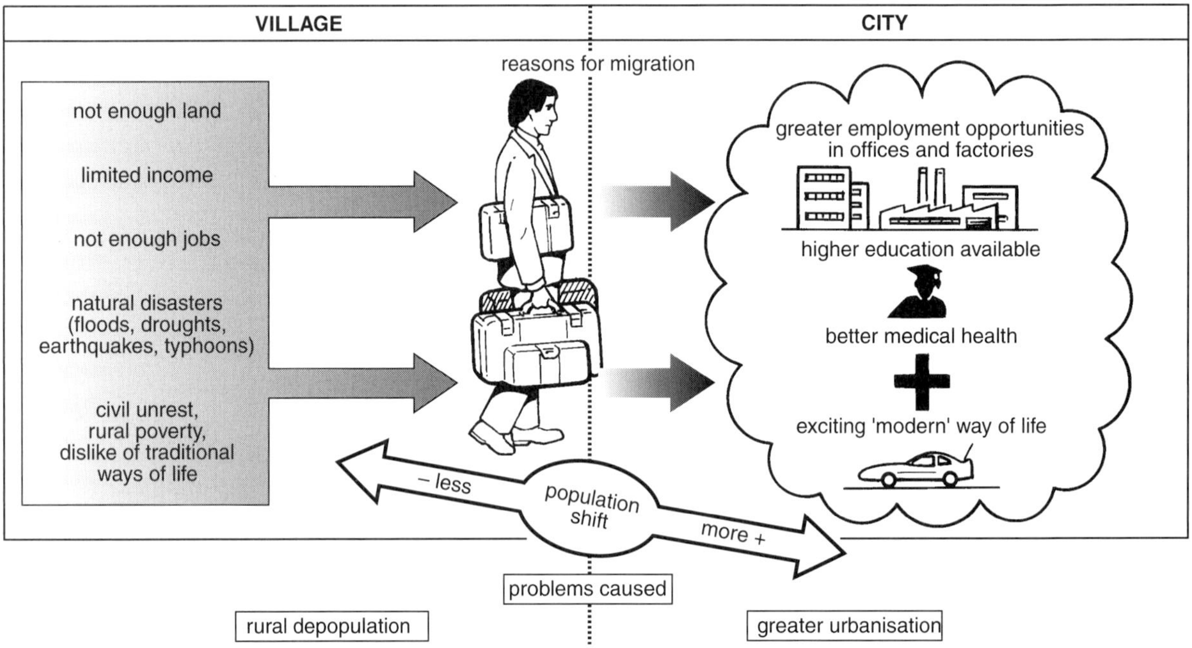

Figure 9.3B Reasons why people migrate

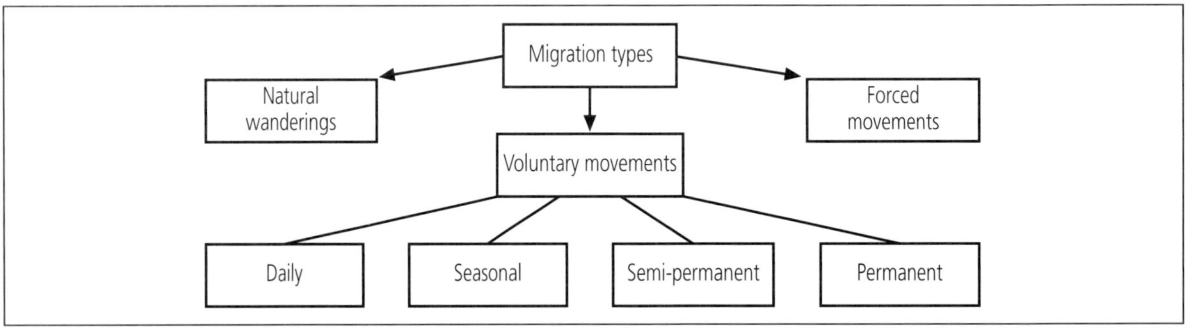

Figure 9.3C Different types of migration

EXTENSION QUESTIONS

4 (a) Study Figure 9.4A which shows population density.

i. State the meaning of the term 'population density'. (2)

ii. Use named examples to help you describe the distribution of areas with high population density. (5)

iii. Use named examples to help you explain the distribution of areas with low population density. (5)

(b) Examine Figure 9.4B which shows some of the factors which influence population density.
For an area of high population density you have studied explain why the population density is high. (7)

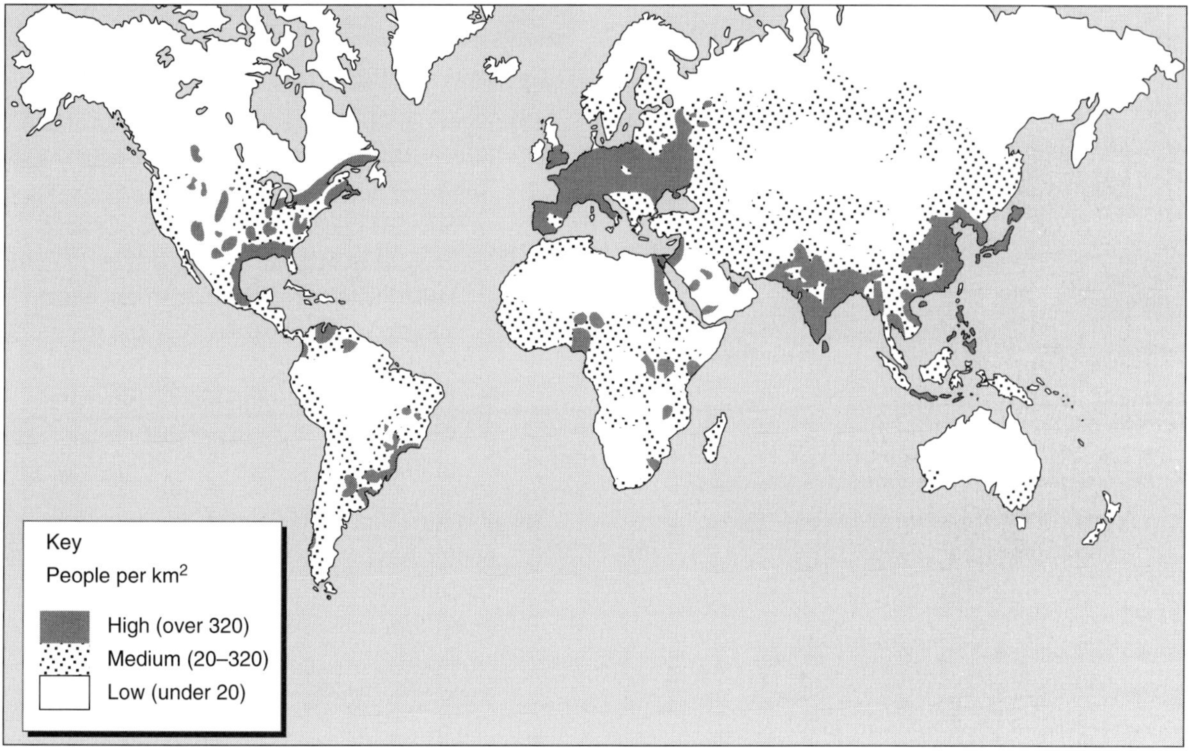

Figure 9.4A Population density

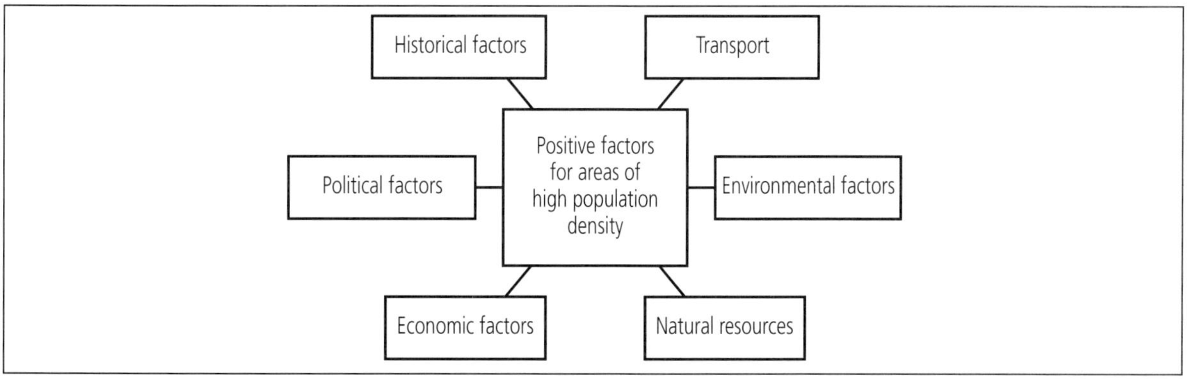

Figure 9.4B Factors which influence population density

(c) Figure 9.4C shows an area of high population density. Discuss the problems which might arise because of high population density in areas such as the one shown in the photograph. (6)

(25)

Figure 9.4C An area of high population density

Figure 9.5B An area of high out-migration

5 (a) Figure 9.5A shows a model of migration. Describe and explain the movements indicated by the model. (4)

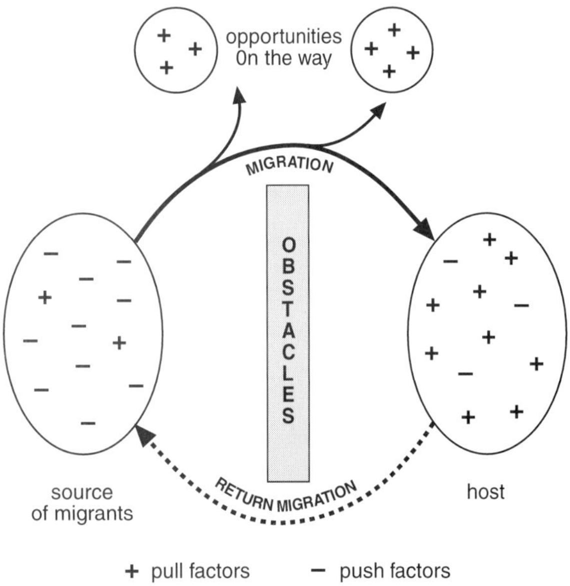

Figure 9.5A A model of migration

(b) Figure 9.5B shows a photograph of an area of high out-migration in an economically developed country.

i. Suggest reasons why some people have decided to migrate from this area. (3)

ii. Describe the problems which can affect an area which experiences high out-migration. (3)

iii. What problems sometimes arise in areas which receive a large number of migrants? (3)

(c) Examine Figure 9.5C which shows population growth for six cities. Account for the differences in the rate of population growth for these six cities. (4)

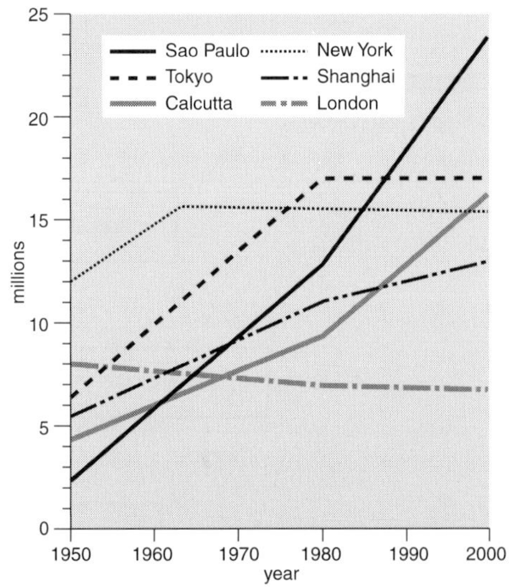

Figure 9.5C Population growth for six cities

> The world's great cities are growing rapidly. In 1900 one tenth of the world's population lived in cities. Today over half the world's population lives in cities and in thirty years time as much as three-quarters of the world's population will be living in cities. Urban growth is greatest in economically developing countries such as Brazil and Egypt where millions of people move, every year, from their homes in the countryside to new lives in the city. But many cities in the poor world cannot cope with the new arrivals and....

Figure 9.5D A newspaper extract

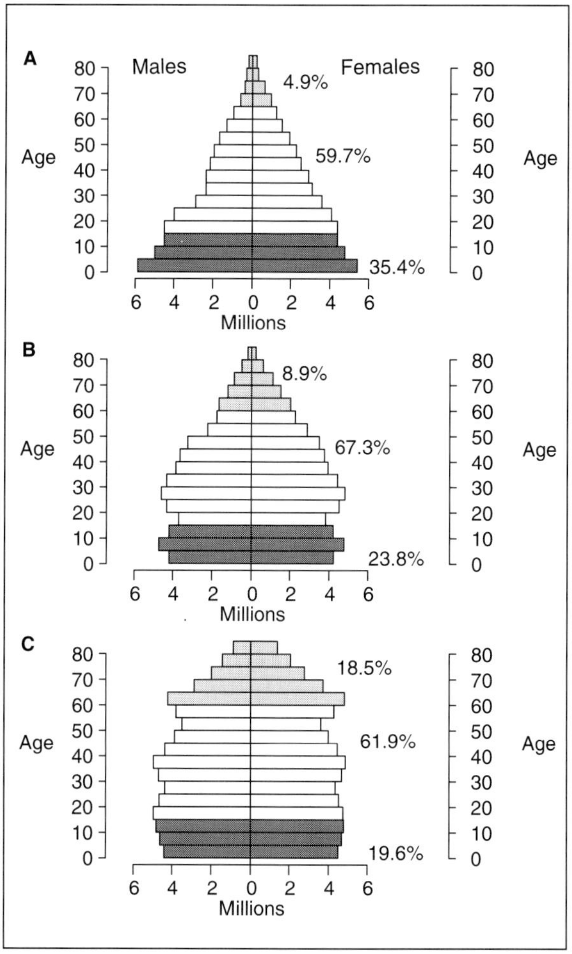

Figure 9.6A Three population pyramids

(d) Using Figure 9.5D describe and explain the problem outlined in the extract. (4)

(e) What is a refugee? Use named examples of refugee movements to help you give a detailed answer. (4)

(25)

6 (a) Using Figure 9.6A, describe which population pyramid (A, B or C) shows:

i. an ageing population; (1)

ii. a youthful population; (1)

iii. a population with high immigration of young adult males? (1)

(b) i.What does 'overpopulation' mean? (2)

ii. What are the causes of overpopulation?(4)

iii. How does overpopulation affect a country?(4)

iv. What can be done to reduce overpopulation in a country like India? (6)

(c) Figure 9.6B shows the relationship between female literacy and estimated population growth.

Describe and account for this relationship. (6)

(25)

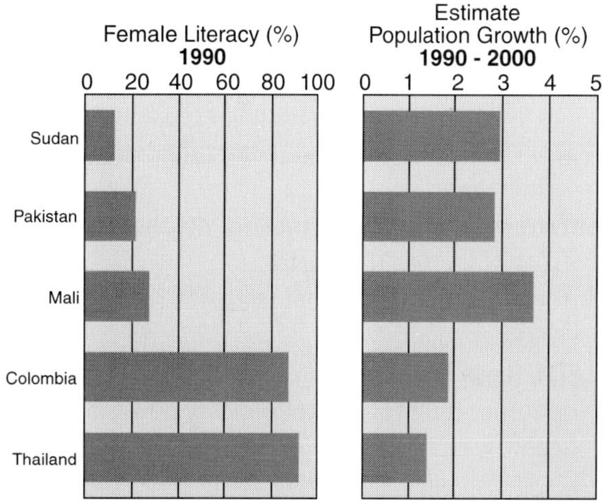

Figure 9.6B The relationship between female literacy and estimated population growth

10 Development issues

Key words

aid the help given by richer countries to poorer countries; aid may consist of food, medical supplies, technology or money

colony a country controlled by another country (the colonial power)

core areas areas lying in the centre of a region which are often more developed, and more prosperous, than areas lying on the periphery

desertification the process of land becoming a desert

economically developed countries rich countries, such as the USA and Japan, which have well developed economies and high living standards

economically developing countries poor countries, such as Bangladesh and Zaire, which have less well developed economies and low living standards

Gross National Product (GNP) the total value of the goods and services produced by a country; figures for GNP are often used as indicators of development

indicators of development statistics which help to indicate a country's standard of living; examples include GNP, literacy rate and life expectancy

infant mortality the number of deaths in the first year of life per 1000 births

international aid aid sent from one country to another country

LEDC (Less Economically Developed Country) another term for an economically developing country

life expectancy the average number of years a new born baby can expect to live

literacy the ability to read and write

MEDC (More Economically Developed Country) another term for an economically developed country

Newly Industrialising Country (NIC) a country, such as South Korea, which has experienced rapid industrial and economic development during the past thirty years

North-South difference the difference between the more economically developed countries of the northern hemisphere and the less economically developed countries of the southern hemisphere

peripheral areas areas lying on the edge of a region which are often less developed, and less prosperous, than areas lying in the core

quality of life the state of well-being of people in a country; quality of life is usually determined by food supply, access to clean water, health care, employment and education

resources materials of value to people, for example: minerals such as oil and coal

self-help scheme a scheme which uses local people, and their skills, to improve conditions in an area

standard of living quality of life

tariff a tax which is put on goods entering a country

technology technical skills and knowledge

tied aid aid with conditions attached

voluntary aid aid which is given without conditions

Figure10.1A An indicator of development

	an economically developing country	**an economically developed country**
Adult literacy rate (percentage of population)	35	99

CORE QUESTIONS

1 (a) Use named examples to help you state the meaning of the following terms:

i. Less Economically Developed Countries (LEDCs). (2)

ii. More Economically Developed Countries (MEDCs). (2)

(b) Examine Figure 10.1A which shows an indicator of development.

i. Give one reason for the different figures for the economically developing countries and the economically developed countries. (1)

ii. State two other indicators of development. (2)

(c) Study Figure 10.1B which shows life expectancy for six countries.

i. State the meaning of the term 'life expectancy'. (1)

ii. Give reasons why life expectancy varies between countries. (4)

iii. Outline ways in which life expectancy can be increased in an economically developing country. (4)

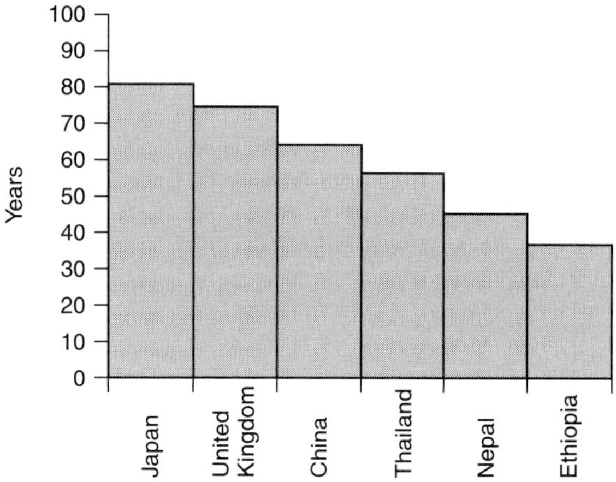

Figure 10.1B Life expectancy for six countries

(d) Study Figure 10.1C which shows four examples of aid to an economically developing country.
Outline how each of these examples of aid will help to improve conditions in an economically developing country. (4)

(20)

Figure 10.1C Four examples of aid to an economically developing country

2 (a) Examine Figure 10.2A which gives information about two families.

Table 10.2A Information about two families

The Getu Family from Ethiopia

Number of people in family	10 (2 adults and 8 children)
Number of rooms in house	1
Most valuable possessions	1 ox, 1 radio and 6 cooking utensils
Annual family income	110 US dollars
Working week	95 hours (for the adults) 30–50 hours (for the children)

The Ford Family from the United States

Number of people in family	3 (2 adults and 1 child)
Number of rooms in house	7
Most valuable possessions	2 cars, 2 TV sets and 2 computers
Annual family income	72 000 US dollars
Working week	36–45 hours (for the adults) 0 hours (for the child)

i. Which family lives in an LEDC? Give two reasons for your choice. (3)

ii. Which family has the better diet? Give two reasons for your choice. (3)

iii. Which country is more likely to provide the best schooling? Give two reasons for your choice. (3)

(b) Figure 10.2B shows the village of Musha in Egypt after the construction of the Aswan Dam.

i. Outline the benefits of the Aswan Dam for the people of Musha. (3)

ii. State one possible disadvantage of the dam for the people of Musha. (1)

(c) Figure 10.2C shows the percentage of population with access to safe drinking water for two LEDCs.

i. Why is there such a big difference between the figures for urban and rural areas? (1)

ii. Why do so many people have no access to safe drinking water? (3)

iii. What can be done to improve the supply of clean water in LEDCs? (3)

(20)

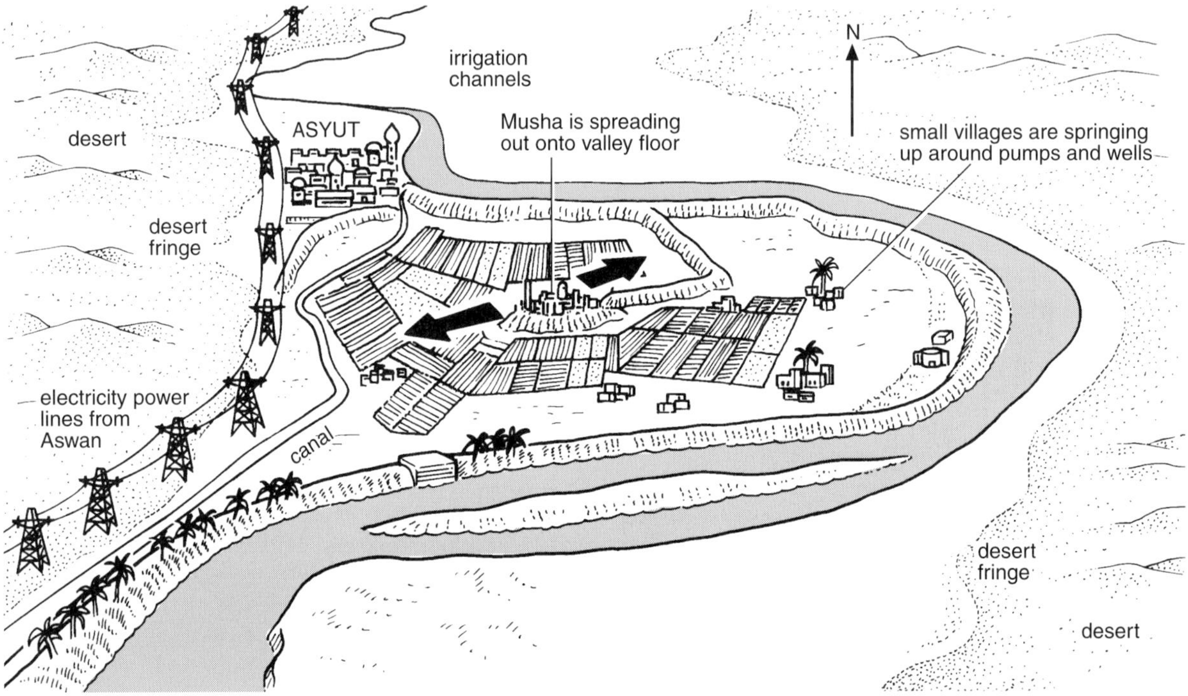

Figure 10.2B The village of Musha

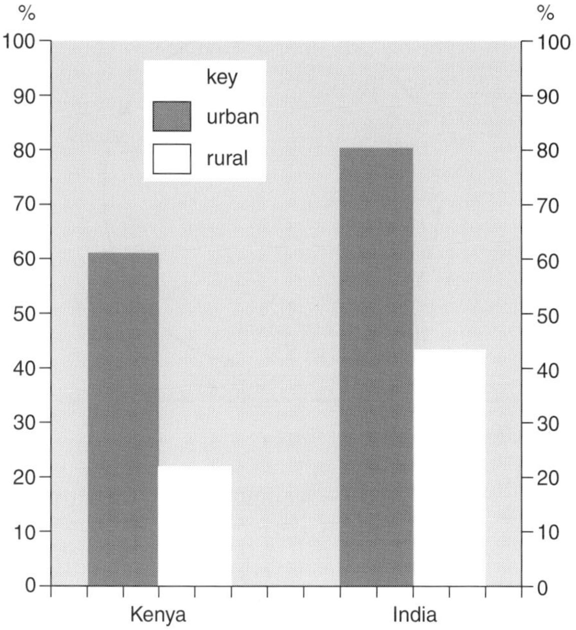

Figure 10.2C The percentage of population with access to safe drinking water

EXTENSION QUESTIONS

3 **(a)** Figure 10.3A shows a poor part of a city in an LEDC while Figure 10.3B shows a rich part of the same city.

i. Describe the different housing conditions which exist in cities in LEDCs. (4)

Figure10.3A A poor part of a city

Figure 10.3B A rich part of a city

ii. Apart from differences in housing what other inequalities exist within LEDCs? Outline three different inequalities. (4)

(b) Study Figure 10.3C which shows four social indicators of living standards.

Infant mortality One in six children dies before the age of five in some of the poorest LEDCs. In MEDCs fewer than one in 50 children die before the age of 5.
Food One quarter of the world's population, mostly in LEDCs, don't have enough food to eat. In many MEDCs many people eat too much and are overweight.
Number of patients per doctor In many LEDCs there is only one doctor for every 4000 people and many people living in villages don't have the transport which is necessary to visit a doctor. In MEDCs there is one doctor for every 400 people and most people who require treatment receive treatment.
Education Children in MEDCs go to school for an average of 11 years. In LEDCs many children are only able to attend school for three or four years and large numbers of children never attend school at all.

Figure 10.3C Four social indicators of living standards

i. With reference to any two of these indicators outline what can be done to improve living standards in LEDCs. (6)

ii. State two economic indicators which could be used to judge the quality of life in a country. (2)

(c) Examine Figure 10.3D which shows the cycle of poverty in less economically developed countries.
Discuss ways in which this cycle of poverty can be broken. (4)

(d) 'Poor water equals poor health.'
Use named examples to help you discuss the accuracy of this statement. (5)

(25)

4 (a) Examine Figure 10.4A which shows Gross National Product (GNP).

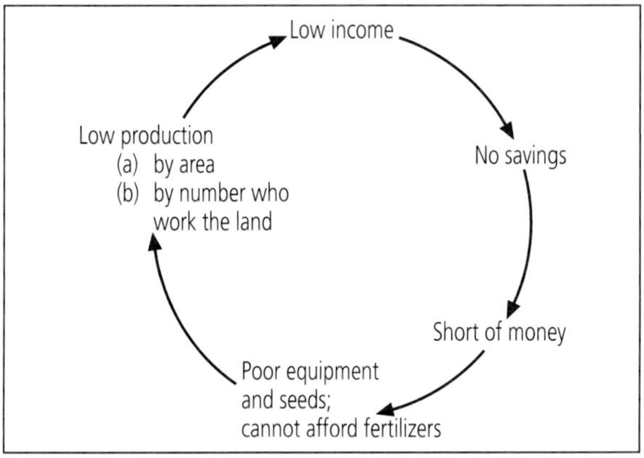

Figure 10.3D The cycle of poverty

i. Outline the meaning of the term 'Gross National Product'. (1)

ii. Give two reasons why GNP is often used as an indicator of a country's development. (2)

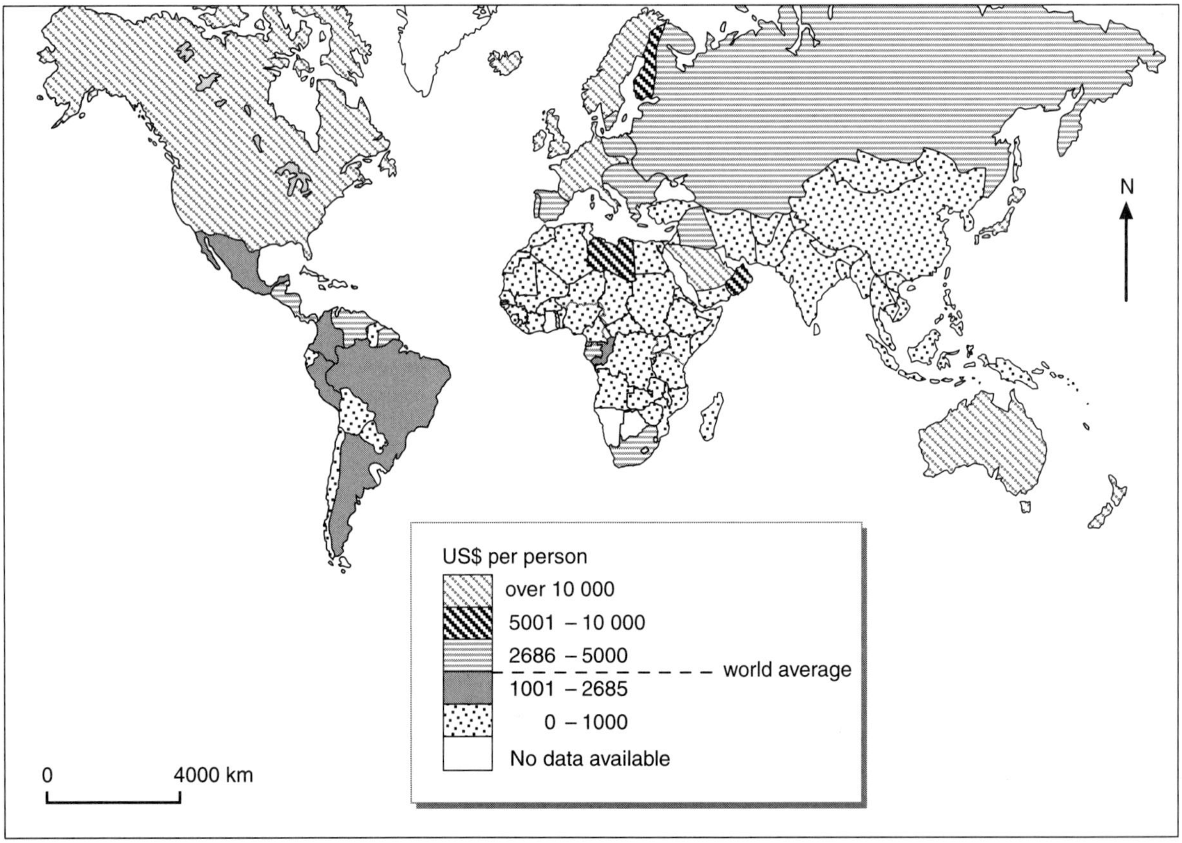

Figure 10.4A Gross National Product

iii. Describe and explain the pattern of GNP shown by Figure 10.4A. (5)

iv. Outline the problems of using GNP as an indicator of a country's development. (3)

v. Apart from GNP what other indicators provide evidence of a country's development? Give one economic indicator and one social indicator of development. (2)

(b) Figure 10.4B shows a model of health care.

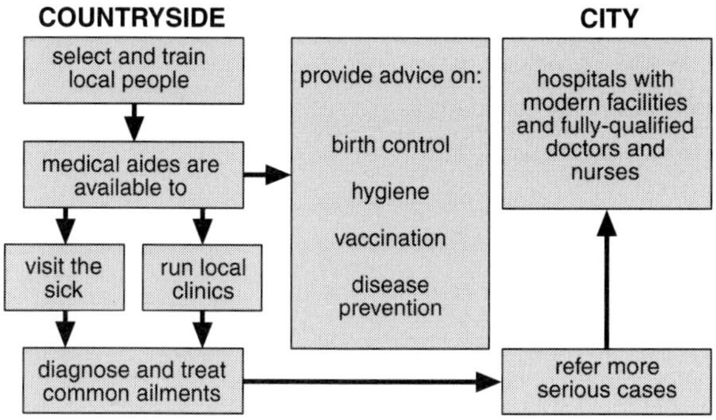

Figure 10.4B A model of health care

i. Assess the usefulness of this system of health care for a rural area in an economically developing country. (3)

ii. Outline other measures which can be taken to improve health care in economically developing countries. (3)

(c) 'Babies born in economically developing countries have a much smaller chance of survival than babies born in economically developed countries.'

i. Explain why child mortality rates are so high in economically developing countries. (3)

ii. Outline measures which would help to reduce child mortality rates in economically developing countries. (3)

(25)

Exam advice

Finally, here is some advice for answering exam questions:

- look at the number of marks for each question – questions with more marks require longer and more-detailed answers;
- look for the key instructions in a question – do exactly what the key instructions command – do not, for example, describe when asked to explain;
- include actual examples and case-studies in your answer – especially if the question instructs you to do this;
- keep your answers relevant to the question – you will waste valuable time if you include irrelevant details.

KEY INSTRUCTIONS IN EXAM QUESTIONS

account give reasons for
annotate add labels
assess weigh up the importance of
comment summarise the various points and give an opinion
compare outline the similarities and differences
contrast highlight the differences
describe state the main features or characteristics
discuss give different points of view
examine look closely
explain give reasons
identify point out and name
locate state where a place is
outline note the main features
quote map evidence give examples, including grid references if possible, from a map
select choose
suggest put forward an idea or reason

HOW TO ANSWER AN EXAM QUESTION

Note that this question has three key instructions:

1 you have to refer to the map (by, for example, including grid references);
2 you have to describe the location of the CBD of York;
3 you have to explain the location of the CBD of York.

- Note that six marks are available for this question: three marks will be awarded for describing the location of the CBD and three marks will be awarded for explaining the location of the CBD. Marks will be deducted if no reference is made to Map 2.

> Use Map 2 to help you describe and explain the location of the central business district of York.
> (6 marks)

- Make sure that your answer only includes sentences and passages which are relevant to the question
- Six marks means that you must write an answer which is around six sentences long and contains at least six points.

WORKED EXAMPLES

Question: 1(c)i. – page 20

Outline the problems which would arise if a major earthquake was to occur in an urban area. (3 marks)

Answer: Urban areas are crowded areas where many people live and work. An earthquake in an urban area would cause much damage to houses, factories, roads and railways. People would be trapped, injured and killed in damaged buildings, cars and trains. There would also be damaged electricity lines and gas pipes which might result in fires and explosions. Broken water pipes would make it difficult to put these fires out.

Marker's comments: This is a well-written answer which gives enough details to earn all 3 marks.

Question: 6(d). – page 34

Figure 2.6C shows the results of a river survey. Describe and explain this data. (6 marks)

Answer: The results of the survey show that water is flowing more slowly at the inner bend and faster in the middle and outer bend of the river. At sample point 1, in the inner bend, the speed is 22 cm/sec compared with 56 cm/sec at point 2 in the middle of the river and 80 cm/sec at sample point 3 in the outer bend. This is because the water is shallower at the inner bend and there is more friction to slow the water down. At the outer bend the water is deeper and there is less friction so the water moves faster.

Marker's comments: This is a reasonable answer which earns four marks. Additional marks would have been earned if the answer had included information about the different depths of the river and how the depth of the river is linked to the speed of the flowing water.

Question: 1(c)i. – page 36

Figure 3.1B shows a photograph of a coastal area. Describe two physical features of this coastal area which make it suitable for tourism. (4 marks)

Answer: Two physical features which make this coastal area suitable for tourism are the bay and the cliffs.

Marker's comments: This answer is too short and only receives 2 marks. Two extra marks would have been awarded if the answer contained additional information about the bay (for example it provides a sheltered area for boats) and the cliffs (for example they are high enough to provide interesting walks and good views over the bay).

Question: 3(c)i. – page 44

What is meant by the term 'tourist honeypot'? (2 marks)

Answer: A 'tourist honeypot' is a place which attracts many visitors and tourists.

Marker's comments: This answer only earns 1 mark because it only provides one point. A second mark would have been awarded if more information about the term 'tourist honeypot' had been provided or if an actual example of a 'tourist honeypot' had been given.

Question: 2(b)iii. – page 51

Explain the weather conditions being experienced at F. (2 marks)

Answer: The weather at F will be wet and windy.

Marker's comments: This response doesn't receive any marks because it doen't answer the question. The question requires an explanation of the weather – not a description. The weather is wet and windy because of the low pressure (which brings unsettled weather) and the presence of a cold front (which brings cloud and rain).

Question: 5(a)i. – page 60

Figure 6.5A shows how land-use changes from the centre of a city to the rural-urban fringe.
Describe the changes in land-use from the central business district to the rural-urban fringe.
(3 marks)

Answer: In the central business district, the main land-uses are offices, shops (including department stores) and roads. In the inner city, the main land-uses are older housing and factories mixed in together. There are fewer shops and offices in this part of the city. In the suburbs, the main land-use is housing.

Marker's comments: This answer provides enough detail to earn all 3 marks.

Question: 1(c). – page 66

During the past 250 years the 'best location' for a steelworks has changed from woodland areas to coalfields to coastal sites. Give reasons for these changes. (3 marks)

Answer: The first iron and steelworks were built next to woodland areas because of the availability of wood which was used in the smelting process. The development of technology led to the use of coal for power and the movement of steelworks to areas which had large supplies of coal and iron-ore. In recent years coal and iron-ore supplies have been worked out and so new steelworks have been built next to the coast where foreign coal and iron-ore can be imported.

Marker's comments: This is a good answer which is worth the full 3 marks.

Question: 4(a). – page 79

Describe the site and situation of Brecks Farm (598567) on the map on the inside back cover.
(4 marks)

Answer: The site of the farm is low land lying at a height of less that 20 metres. The site of the farm is also flat land. The farm is situated next to a small stream a few kilometres to the north of York. The farm is also situated next to the B1363 road not far from its junction with the A1237 main road.

Marker's comments: This answer, although quite short in length, contains enough detail to earn all 4 marks.

Question: 6(b)iii. – page 87

How does overpopulation affect a country? (4 marks)

Answer: Overpopulation will cause many problems for a country. Unemployment will be high and this may lead to lower living standards. In farming communities some people will have no land for growing food. Malnutrition and starvation will occur when families don't have any money or any means of growing food. Other families will have incomes which are so low that they can't afford to buy enough food, clothes and other basic requirements. Malnutrition and disease are major problems in many parts of the world which are overpopulated.

Marker's comments: This answer provides enough detail to earn all 4 marks.

Question: 4(a)iv. – page 93

Examine Figure 10.4A which shows Gross National Product (GNP). Outline the problems of using GNP as an indicator of a country's development. (3 marks)

Answer: GNP is an average figure which can hide great differences in wealth within a country.

Marker's comments: This answer is too short, and lacking in detail, to earn more than 1 mark. Other marks would have been given for providing an example of a GNP figure which hides great differences in wealth within a country.